The Gurus, the Mountain and the Silence

Tales from Tiruvannamalai

The Gurus, the Mountain and the Silence

Tales from Tiruvannamalai

Subhuti Anand Waight

First published in 2020 by CinnamonTeal Design & Publishing

ISBN: 978–93–87676–75–6

Author's website: www.subhutianand.com

Typesetting and Cover design: CinnamonTeal Design and Publishing

Portrait Illustrations: Aniket Naik

CinnamonTeal Design & Publishing
Plot No 16, Housing Board Colony
Gogol, Margao
Goa 403601 India
www.cinnamonteal.in

To those who climb the mountain.

Go back to that state of pure being,
Where the 'I am' is still in its state of purity
Before it got contaminated with 'I am this' or 'I am that.'
Your burden is of false identifications – abandon them all.

Contents

INTRODUCTION
THE MYSTIC AND THE MOUNTAIN

In the half-light of dawn, I leave the road and turn down a narrow lane that is almost hidden in the dark shadow of the ashram's rear wall. This, so I'm told, is the path that leads to the steps that will take me up the mountain. This is how one can avoid waiting for the ashram's rear gate to open and make an early start for the caves.

But there is a potential hazard ahead. Three curled shapes, lying on the path, inform me that this is the territory of several street dogs. Or maybe they belong to families now soundly sleeping in the row of tiny houses facing the ashram wall.

Will they let me pass without a fuss? Or will they put on a spectacular show for the neighbourhood by barking madly and blocking my path? I try to walk in a relaxed and casual manner, as if I do this every morning.

"Hey, it's okay." I'm telling them. "I'm just part of the scenery. No need to kick up a fuss."

None of them so much as twitches an ear. Clearly, 6:00 am in the morning is not their favourite time to become hysterical about strangers. The houses fade away behind me and, sure enough, the path brings me to the ashram's back gate which usually remains locked until around 8:00 am. The steps to the caves begin here. Slowly I start to climb.

There's nobody around. The beggars, the sadhus, the water and fruit sellers who line the trail in daytime are not yet at their stations. No customers at this hour. Even though it's half-dark, the steps are well-formed so easy to navigate. There are trees on either side and somewhere off to my right a monkey or a bird gives a harsh cry followed by a deepening silence.

I walk steadily up the pathway and within a few minutes arrive at a painting, made on three slabs of flat rock, showing Ramana Maharshi sitting amid abundant nature. It's an appeal to help fund the reforestation project that gives Arunachala its green canopy and wildlife.

This, too, is the place where, in days gone by, an inner circuit of Arunachala would have normally begun. Being a holy mountain, a manifestation of Shiva himself, Arunachala is regarded by the Hindu faithful as a temple to walk around.

Every fullmoon night, thousands of pilgrims walk the 12-kilometre *girivalam* route, usually beginning and ending at the gates of Ramana Ashram. Pradakshina, as it's also known, forms the outer ring around Arunachala and is now a well-paved, brightly lit, circular road with cafés, restaurants, dozens of temples – and just about anything you can imagine on sale.

There used to be an inner path, popular with Westerners, that wove its way through the woods, also circumnavigating the mountain, well away from traffic and crowds. As a matter of fact, it's still here, but has been placed out of bounds by

  Subhuti Anand Waight

the police. Alas, increasing popularity has brought serious problems: harassment of women, robbery and worse.

I continue up the main path and note that the sky is becoming lighter. Soon, the sun will poke its red nose over the horizon and the cool mountain air will rapidly warm as temperatures soar towards the thirty mark – and beyond.

After half-an-hour of steady walking, with almost no view at all, I come out into the open, standing on an outcrop of rock. From here, you can look down on the town of Tiruvannamalai and on Arunachaleswara, the massive Shiva temple that dominates its centre.

It was in this temple that Ramana, as a young man, lay in deep trance, as if dead, while mice nibbled his feet and ants bit his legs. He was discovered and removed by well-wishers and thereafter escorted around locally from temple to temple, place to place, eventually choosing to live in caves on the mountain.

The view from here is spectacular and I share the panorama with a pair of huge birds, either buzzards or eagles, passing silently overhead, cruising on the updrafts, gliding effortlessly around Arunachala's slopes, no doubt looking for an early breakfast.

Now my journey is no longer uphill. From this point, the path levels off and then descends slightly. Suddenly, when Skandashram is almost in sight, a small troop of red-faced monkeys make their presence felt, skittering around amid the trees off to my left.

They eye me speculatively, looking for signs that I'm carrying food. It's an ingrained habit, for which they can be forgiven, because a woman often sits here during the daytime selling bananas to pilgrims so they can feed them to the monkeys, while taking photos on their mobile phones. She's not here yet and I have no scrap of food to offer.

"No luck, guys!" I announce cheerfully, but keep a nervous eye on them as I pass. Monkeys can be fun. They can also be very bad news, especially if you get bitten by one. Then a whole series of anti-rabies shots and other precautions need to be taken.

The monkeys lose interest in me and after a couple of minutes I arrive at Skandashram, the cave where Ramana lived for seven years after coming to Arunachala. Here, he was joined by his mother who meditated with him and began preparing meals for him. This was a practical necessity since Ramana showed no interest in eating unless he was invited to do so.

There is a sweet little story about a small boy who, walking on the mountain near his home, unexpectedly came upon Ramana, sitting on a rock, doing nothing.

"Why are you here all alone like this?" asked the boy.

"I had some trouble at home, so I have come away like this," answered Ramana.

"Then how about your food?" asked the boy.

"I eat if anybody gives me anything to eat," the mystic replied.

Concerned, the boy offered his help in finding Ramana a job, so he could earn wages and feed himself. Obligingly, the mystic agreed, but, of course, it never happened.

So, Ramana's devoted followers had to make sure food was available. When his mother died, Ramana declared that she had become enlightened. Her *mahasamadhi* is next to his own, down in the ashram below.

As I expected, Skandashram is locked at this hour and will remain so until 8:15 am, when the custodians, now still sleeping inside the walls, will open the gates to the public. I could wait here for that to happen. But I'm not especially interested in going inside, which I did on a previous trek up the mountain. Nor do I feel pulled to walk down to the second cave, Virupakshi, where Ramana also lived.

My attraction to Arunachala isn't focused on special places. It's a more general feeling of "at homeness," as if the mountain radiates an energy field that welcomes seekers and meditators, making them feel they are close to the source. Certainly, this is what pulled Ramana to Arunachala. He used to say that the mountain's power had been generated by the hundreds of yogis, *sadhus* and *siddhas* who had meditated here, in centuries gone by.

In fact, there's a lovely myth: Deep inside Arunachala, in a golden cave, Ramana still sits, surrounded by enlightened rishis and saints, who are all immersing themselves in pure consciousness, then emanating its light to the world. Nice story. Not factual, of course, but as a spiritual metaphor it contains a truth that can be felt by anyone who comes here to meditate.

Today, though, I'm not looking for the golden cave. I'm eyeing the path to the top of the mountain which begins in front of Skandashram, then winds its way across a rock face and disappears up the hill.

Climbing the mountain to the top is not really allowed. Once again, the police have felt it necessary to intervene ever since a tourist, injured in a fall, was unable to make his way down, and died. But the ban is only loosely enforced. Most of the time, there's no police around to prevent anyone from making the upward pilgrimage.

I know there's no real point in climbing to the top. The invitation that Arunachala offers, to each one of us, is to look inward, to climb the inner mountain of consciousness and claim the eternal treasure of the Self.

Still, it's a lovely morning and there's nobody around. It is tempting…

THE TAO OF THE TRANSFER

She was blonde, good-looking and as helpful as an airport official could be. But, alas, she couldn't prevail against a computerized check-in system that would not deliver.

"I don't think you're going to make it," she said, sympathetically, handing me back my boarding pass.

For over half-an-hour, I'd been occupying one of the desks at the Air India check-in, at Copenhagen Airport. I'm surprised the other passengers, waiting in line behind me, didn't start screaming their frustration. Two friends, checking in with me, had waited patiently for ten minutes, then signalled they were going through security. I didn't blame them.

The blonde had already called her supervisor, an efficient-looking, clean shaven young SAS official who looked like he should have been modelling for an after-shave commercial.

Together, this pair looked like the dream Danish couple.

He tried. She tried. They tried together. They consulted a manual. They entered all kinds of codes, but the computer system defeated them. They called their super-supervisor, a fiercely-intelligent-looking female executive on a posting from Air India head office in Delhi. She possessed high tech savvy, plus powers intended to override any problem. Except this one.

The problem was I'd bought a flight ticket from Copenhagen to Delhi and then, a few weeks later, added a connecting domestic flight from Delhi to Chennai. Both were with Air India, but the system refused to merge them. Why? Because of a glitch called "Name Mismatch."

Dumb dude that I was, I'd added a middle name to one ticket and not the other. Fail.

The super-supervisor applied her override powers. Fail.

She called head office in Delhi. Fail.

Apologetically, they handed back my original boarding pass. This meant that on arrival at Indira Gandhi Airport in Delhi, I'd have to make a complete exit from Terminal Three, then re-enter and check in all over again, instead of passing through the much speedier internal transfer route. The time between my two flights would be very short.

The trip to Delhi was uneventful. As to be expected with Air India's low budget status, the movies were old and the Asian Veg meal looked even older, but I'm pleased to say our flight was comfortable and swift.

Proudly, the captain announced, "I'm happy to tell you we are arriving 20 minutes early."

Good news! But then, in its shadow, came bad news.

"I'm sorry to tell you our docking bay is not ready," he added.

Worse was to come. The tourist promotion movie on our seat-back screens portrayed Delhi as a city with clean air and bright, sunny skies. But, alas, the grey fog outside the plane windows told a different story. Due to a severe attack of early morning pollution, we were re-assigned to "a remote area" of the airport. Buses may or may not be coming within 10-15 minutes, we were informed.

"I'm doomed," I muttered to myself. This had been the extra time I'd needed in order not to panic.

Suddenly, though, people were moving, the plane was emptying and soon I found myself in a bus. Wow, how did that happen so fast? In Copenhagen, it took ages for some of these well-rounded, middle-aged Indian ladies in saris to shuffle aboard the plane and now they were almost running like greyhounds out of the starting trap.

The bus dropped us at Arrivals and I raced to Immigration. It was a long, gleaming, white hall with endless desks and, praise be, it was almost empty! Unfortunately, it was also almost empty of immigration officials.

I saw the e-visa sign: lots of desks, but only one was manned. Never mind, I have somehow managed to be second in line. The couple in front were taking forever to be processed and were required to give digital fingerprints, by resting their fingers and thumbs on top of a small, green-lit box.

When it was my turn, the guy stamped my passport and casually waved me through.

"No fingerprint?" I asked in surprise, my curiosity temporarily suppressing my need for haste.

"You are a senior citizen!" he said with a smile and gave me a mock salute of approval.

My god! So, old, white, Englishmen are not an international security risk it seems.

I grabbed my suitcase off the baggage belt and exited Terminal Three into the cold gloomy haze of Delhi's cheerless morning, then quickly re-entered through Departures.

As I feared, it was a madhouse. Polite queues are not a natural part of Indian culture. They must have been imposed by British colonialists. Queues appear to exist, but in name

   Subhuti Anand Waight

only. In reality, it's a question of who can push their way to the desk and shout the loudest.

I spotted a capable-looking official with a security pass hanging around his neck. He seemed to have time on his hands and, like all of us, might be in need of an extra buck.

"I'm going to miss my flight!" I pleaded.

He nodded, took my trolley, guided me all the way to the far end of the Air India check-in area, where he somehow found a desk and got me checked in.

Great! Of course, he deserved a reward. But I had no rupee notes. Carelessly, I'd left them in the UK before travelling to Copenhagen. All I had were GBP ten-pound notes, each worth 800 rupees. It was way too much for a tip, but, hey, he saved my life. Have a nice day.

Security was next and to my dismay I viewed long lines, strictly enforced by strips of crowd-controlling belts that zig-zagged forever into the distance. These narrow corridors were crammed with people and my heart sank. The clock was ticking.

Summoning my acting skills and playing the helpless tourist for the second time in ten minutes, I breathlessly approached a female police officer and held out my boarding pass.

"I'm worried that I'll miss my flight!" I exclaimed.

Glancing at my boarding time, she was not impressed.

"You'll make it," she said and nodded towards the line. No fast-track with this lady.

Joining the line at the very end, I reflected for a moment on the foolishness of my panic-stricken attitude. I was acting as if catching this plane was a life-or-death issue. How absurd! I'd come here to India to meditate, feel inner peace, let go of worldly attachments.

I was on my way to the ashram of Ramana Maharshi, a mystic so detached from worldly affairs he wouldn't bother to brush an ant off his skin, even if it was biting him. Also, I was well aware there were two more Air India flights to Chennai that afternoon, so even if I missed this one I'd still make it to Tiruvannamalai by tonight.

Calmed by this voice of reason, I took several deep breath and forced myself to relax, surrendering to my fate. Then, suddenly, up ahead, I saw my two travel companions from Copenhagen, standing very close to the security X-ray machines. They'd been able to go the fast way through internal transfer.

I hesitated for a moment, then, throwing spiritual detachment aside, I ducked through half-a-dozen tapes to join them, expecting someone to shout at me. Nobody did. In India, jumping lines seems to be tolerated more than elsewhere because everyone knows that with these crowds, catching planes can be a hazardous, last-minute affair.

Going through security, I almost lost my boarding pass, while cramming my belongings into small blue trays that slid away from me on the rolling track. Then I found myself standing on a small box, arms raised, while a policeman briskly caressed my entire body with a looped metal detector.

In the world of BDSM, this might be considered a kind of fetish. How many times did he need to pass that thing over my buttocks? Eventually, the bored cop stamped my boarding pass and nodded me through.

I was making good progress now, on my way to Gate 29A, but Terminal Three seemed as vast as Delhi itself. Large video screens showed images of relaxed, smiling young travellers, all informing me how efficient and modern this terminal is. How nice of them.

It was a long, long walk, but on arrival I found the gate has not yet opened. The boarding schedule was late. There was even time for a cup of coffee and my very first 'veg puff' of my stay in India. As usual, one bite of this savoury pastry – found at every airport – sent powdery flakes showering all over my pants. But I didn't care. I made it!

 Subhuti Anand Waight

THINK I'M GONNA LIKE IT HERE

Our taxi skirts around the town of Tiru, drives past the gates of the Ramana Ashram, heads towards the setting sun for a couple of kilometres, then deposits us outside a guest house.

From my immediate impressions, I can already feel I don't like Tiru. It's too busy, too noisy, too polluted with traffic fumes. But I also know, from long personal experience as a wandering nomad, that I never like anywhere at first glance.

For reasons unknown – maybe rooted in some past life, while wandering with Moses in the desert, looking for the Promised Land – my first take on a place is always: "This isn't what I'm looking for. Let's get out of here!"

Instead of following this impulse, I take a few deep breaths, tell myself to relax, note the splendid view of Mount Arunachala from outside my apartment, and enjoy a warm hug with my welcoming friend Gayatri – like me she has adopted an Indian name – who has kindly arranged my stay.

Thank god for friends who know the local scene because if I'd arrived in Tiru as a complete newcomer, at the beginning of January during peak tourist season, it would have been hard to find a place. But Gayatri, my Dutch friend and Tiru hostess, has been here several times before. When she cut off her hair recently, her smooth head, sun-darkened skin and enigmatic smile made Gayatri look for all the world like a Tibetan Buddhist nun.

I can see, as she welcomes me, her expression has that timeless, enigmatic quality of someone who likes to live away from the world and all its hustle. She loves Tiru and was kind enough to book me a small apartment just outside of town.

By the way, I had written to the ashram itself and asked to stay inside for a few days, which anyone can do. It's one of the preferred methods of arriving here because you're immediately at the heart of things. It also gives you time to look around for a place outside.

But early January is Ramana's birthday, traditionally celebrated on the first full moon after his actual birth date, and all ashram guest spaces were booked out months ago.

"I hope you like it, there wasn't much choice," says Gayatri apologetically, as we unlock the door of my new home.

I don't like it. It's bare, ugly, harshly lit by neon tubes, and full of mosquitoes. And it's going to cost me 700 rupees a day which was more than I'd budgeted for.

"It was 500 last year, but prices are going up," Gayatri explains. Of course, Tiru is changing. As more and more people hear about it, demand for accommodation increases and so do local dreams of wealth. Visitors like me are making life difficult for visitors like me.

"It's great, thanks!" I tell Gayatri, lying bravely. She gives me another hug, tells me the landlord is on his way and we arrange to meet later for dinner.

          Subhuti Anand Waight

Meanwhile, I set about killing mosquitoes. As I smack them, I look at my hands and see they're covered with blood. The last tenant offered them a real feast. Maybe he left the door open at night, or maybe – horror of horrors – there are gaping holes in the protective netting covering the windows.

My landlord is a short stocky guy, around fifty, with a drooping black moustache which makes him look rather like a Mexican bandit from an old Western movie. He drives a motorbike, wears a white shirt and has no pants. He's local, so he wears a lunghi, or sarong.

He doesn't speak much English, but the universal language of money is understood by both of us. I want to pay him for just one week, hoping to find somewhere better. He wants two weeks, minimum.

Okay, I give in. I hand over 9,800 rupees and we arrange to meet again tomorrow to complete the necessary "C Form," the registration of foreigners required by the police.

I know I won't be able to kill all the mosquitoes by tonight, but that's okay. I've brought a handy-sized mosquito net with me, which I quickly arrange over the bed. I make a mental note to buy one of those electric mosquito zappers, shaped like a tennis racquet, that can zap a mosquito in mid-flight, provided your backhand stroke is as good as Roger Federer's.

I'll also buy a liquid anti-mosquito burner, and if all else fails, I have a large tube of legendary 'Odomos' made-in-India mosquito repellent which we used back in the old days, in the Seventies. Then it was a green-coloured cream and smelled disgusting. Now, it's white with almost no smell. I hope it still works.

In case you haven't got it by now, I have a thing about mosquitoes. It's true, I'm afraid of malaria and the dreaded dengue fever, which is usually non-fatal, but often so painful it makes you wish it was.

My main reason, however, is more mundane: I know, from long experience, one lonely, hungry mosquito can ruin my night's sleep. So, it's part of my welcome-to-India routine to establish, as far as possible, a mosquito-free zone. By the way, as you may have gathered, I'm an old India hand but until now I've never ventured south of Goa.

I've also brought with me a pair of bedsheets and a soft pillow. I'd been warned ahead of time that Tiru landlords often don't supply sheets and, as many travellers know, guest house pillows in India often seem to be filled with concrete.

Okay, with basic survival equipment in place, I strip off and step into the bathroom. The water heater works and the shower head gives a nice spray on my body. That's more than I expected. Often, a cold shower is all that is available in low budget accommodation – and sometimes only a bucket and a tap.

Half-way through the shower I realize I didn't bring a towel and the landlord didn't supply one. Okay, no problem. I have so many layers of clothes, essential while departing from the miserable winter of Denmark, but after arriving in Tiru completely superfluous, so I can use an undershirt to dry myself.

I'll shop for towels tomorrow. One practical tip Gayatri has already given me is to buy a pair of very thin towels. They dry swiftly, even indoors, and you always have one ready for use.

Slipping into a fresh t-shirt and my old blue jeans, I lock up the apartment and head for the ashram. This, I know, is going to be the real test. If I don't like the ashram, I won't be able to stay here more than a couple of days. If I like it, I could be here for months.

I flag down a yellow rickshaw and he drives me into town, dropping me outside the gate. The curving green sign above the entrance announces: "SRI RAMANASRAMAM." In simple English: Ramana Ashram.

Walking in the gate, I'm grateful to feel immediately shielded from the street noise. There's a thick stone wall

     Subhuti Anand Waight

around the whole place which does an effective job in keeping out the world.

I leave my trainers at the shoe kiosk tucked away on the left side of the entrance, and pause to admire the technique of the shoe master. He sits at the counter, pokes the end of a long bamboo stick into my shoe, grasps the other end of the stick, then swivels around and neatly deposits the shoe on a shelf behind him. He does this twice and the job is done. No need to get up from his chair.

I walk gingerly over the sandy gravel into the ashram, shaded by big trees such as almond and coconut palms, and there's a huge bougainvillea, full of purple and pink flowers, blossoming over the office roof.

It's busy here, with people coming and going, but at the same time the general mood seems calm and unhurried. I like the atmosphere, the sense of a sheltered oasis from the madness of daily life.

I'm not sure where I'm heading, but I climb some steps, then turn left into what I later learn is Ramana's mother's samadhi which sits alongside the main hall where Ramana's own samadhi is located. Following the flow of people, I soon find myself walking around the mother's samadhi and then through a side entrance into the main hall.

Still following the crowd, I begin to walk in slow, ritualized circles around Ramana's samadhi, where a group of Brahmin priests and young boys are chanting the Vedas.

The hall is filled with people, women sitting on one side, men on the other. To my surprise, I see a couple of dogs stretched out on the floor enjoying a snooze, while people come and go around them. Nobody tries to kick them out, so obviously they're part of the scenery.

Pretty soon, the Vedic chanting ends and soft singing begins in the hall, with men and women alternating, as if answering each other. It sounds lovely and a lot of people seem to know the words.

It's a promising beginning, but I'm not staying. I have a dinner date with Gayatri and the two women who came with me on the flight. We enjoy a good Indian meal together, then I head home to my apartment.

To my great pleasure, the number of mosquitoes has not increased which means the netting on the windows is okay. Still, on that first night, I slide under my mosquito net and enjoy one hundred percent protection.

Turning out the light, I feel warm, cosy and relaxed, as if coming home after a long journey.

"I think I'm going to like it here" I tell myself. Then fall asleep.

          Subhuti Anand Waight

MOOJI AND THE PIZZA PARLOUR

They are singing in the main hall of Ramana Ashram. I'm standing outside, enjoying the melodic echoes of the male and female voices, watching the evening shadows lengthen -- and thinking about pizza.

I've been on my own all afternoon and now I want company for dinner. There are at least half-a-dozen people inside the hall whom I know, either casually or as friends. Whoever comes out soonest will be my first choice.

Ramana Maharshi, as many people know, popularized the question "Who Am I?" as a form of self-inquiry and self-realization. Today, in moments of solitude, I found myself exploring a variation: "Who am I without people?" No answer came in words, but it was an interesting and slightly scary feeling.

Hannah emerges from the hall. Smiling a warm greeting, she comes to stand beside me. Hannah is German, in her mid-thirties, friendly and forthright, with straw-coloured hair and green eyes. We vaguely know each other having met briefly at a meditation centre in Denmark.

"Shall we have dinner together?" I ask.

"Yes," she replies, "But we need to wait for Marie."

Five minutes later, Marie emerges from the hall. She is also from Germany, tall with dark hair, a little more reserved by nature, but also interested in dinner. We discuss where to go and discover we're all a bit tired of Indian *thali*.

"There's a place near my guest house," I suggest. "They do pizza on Wednesdays and Saturdays."

Hannah and Marie agree. Outside the ashram gate we climb into a rickshaw and speed away through busy traffic. It's getting dark now and the shop lights are twinkling.

Suddenly, Hannah screams in my ear, "Mooji!"

I don't hear it right. I assume she's spotted an old friend.

"Stop! Stop!" she cries to the rickshaw driver.

He is confused, so am I, but, swept along by Hannah's excitement, I tell the drive to pull over and wait. "We come back. We pay you extra for waiting," I assure him, and he seems satisfied. Westerners are anyway crazy.

Hannah is hurrying back down the street and Marie and I follow. There's a small crowd around the gate of a guest house.

"It's Mooji!" cries Hannah breathlessly. "My girlfriend is crazy about him! I've got to get a photo and send it to her."

Now I understand her excitement. She's spotted the Jamaican spiritual teacher here on the street, and that's why we stopped. We join the small crowd surrounding Mooji. There are two or three Western women, all with lovely smiles, seemingly welcoming everyone who accidentally shows up. Like us, for example.

Mooji is saying hello to several Indian men who obviously know him from previous years when he was a regular here

     Subhuti Anand Waight

in Tiru. I'd already heard that Mooji might be in town, visiting the shrine of Ramana his guru, although he probably wouldn't be giving *Satsang* here because he's scheduled to start in Rishikesh.

I take a photo, Hannah takes a photo, but then it occurs to me: "Hey, Hannah, to really impress your girlfriend we should have our photo taken *with* Mooji."

Hannah hesitates, but the man himself seems available, so I take a couple of steps forward and ask, "Mooji, will you be kind enough to allow my friend and I to have our photo taken with you?"

"Of course," he says.

So, we put our arms around each other, like old friends, while Hannah cuddles him shyly from the other side and one of Mooji's beautiful assistants taps rapidly on the screen of my mobile phone. Mooji, I have to say, has a lovely energy. Close up like this, I can feel it.

We thank him, say goodbye, walk back to the rickshaw and check out the pics. To our astonishment, none have been taken. Only the one I took myself. The lovely assistant had tapped the wrong button. Oh well, no going back now.

"It wasn't meant to be," declares Hannah.

We laugh it off and head for the café. I reward the rickshaw driver for his patience by paying him double, then we go in and find a table.

We order pizza. Among a range of fancy names, I opt for a 'Sri Ramana.' All pizzas are vegetarian anyway, which is my main concern, so it doesn't matter which one I choose.

After a few minutes, as we're waiting, there's a mild commotion at the door. We look around. Mooji and an entourage of about ten people are coming for pizza, sitting at a long table next to our own. Unknowingly, it seems we have chosen one of the best tables in the coolest place in town.

The owners and waiters all rush to touch Mooji's feet and welcome him. I guess he's been here before. At this moment, another guy who gives Satsang in Tiru also comes in and takes the table on the other side of us.

We are now in the world's most spiritual pizza parlour.

"I'm glad we made our order before they showed up!" I tell my companions.

The pizza is thinly-crusted and delicious. After eating we stay on, sipping lemon sodas, enjoying the situation and the energy.

I feel relaxed and tired. I walked up the mountain to Ramana's cave today, for the second time since arriving. I also feel mildly blissed out, but whether it's because of Mooji, my two sweet companions, the unlikely events or the effect of the caves, it's hard to say.

Mooji is about to start eating his own pizza when a serious, pale-faced young man walks across to his table and asks for spiritual guidance. Here's where, if it was me, lacking perhaps in unconditional compassion, I'd say, "Hey man, let me eat my pizza in peace!"

But no. A space is made at the table and the young man sits down, holds Mooji's outstretched hand and promptly bursts into tears. We can't hear what's being said, but eventually the young man thanks Mooji and moves away.

The pizza parlour is getting crowded and not everyone is here for the food. When Mooji's party gets up to go, Hannah urges me to ask him to retake the photo with us, but I shake my head.

"Let's not bother the guy," I tell her.

As it is, it's going to take him a long time to get out of the restaurant as the waiters touch his feet once more and the Westerners say "Hi" and take photos.

I guess there's a price to pay for being famous.

                    Subhuti Anand Waight

THE WAITING GAME

In all innocence I seem to have started a movement. Now there is no turning back. Really, it was unintentional. I had been sitting on a stone step outside the library building in Ramana Ashram for the best part of 60 minutes, my poor bony backside suffering patiently.

When my physical discomfort became too great, I stood up to stretch, and that's when a collective misunderstanding rippled through the waiting crowd. They took this as a signal that the doors ahead of us were opening, so everyone stood up and began to press forward, challenging my place in line. Looking unconcerned and casual, I had to spread my legs to stand in such a way that nobody could slip by me.

The situation offered a comical blend of human qualities, as we tried to look spiritual and meditative while competing for prime positions at the same time.

Nochur, a brilliant Brahmin scholar with a long and unpronounceable name – I learned only the first part of it – was giving a series of morning lectures in English. He looked like a traditional Hindu priest, with a wrap-around cotton robe, one shoulder bared and one covered, his head shaved, with three or four broad white stripes across his forehead.

But he was no ordinary priest. He was lively, juicy, passionate, funny, and extremely well educated. His lectures were on Ramana Maharshi, the great man's sayings and life, but Nochur's ideas flowed effortlessly between Ramana, the Upanishads, the Vedas, other saints and seers....

Not only that, he kept bringing us, his audience, back to the essential core of self-inquiry. Not only that, he somehow filled the room with an impersonal presence, at once empty and blissful, as if the vibe of the sacred mountain behind him had been invited into the room, seducing us all into meditation.

Today was Nochur's second lecture and word was out. This was good stuff. Hence the crowd outside the library. I'd come at eight o'clock, was probably tenth in line, and an hour later there was a sizeable gathering behind me.

The library isn't hard to find. Walking in the gate of Ramana Ashram and leaving your shoes in the racks, you simply keep walking straight ahead until finally, at the end of the pathway, the round, modern-looking shape of the library greets you.

Standing here, looking back through the ashram, I see more and more people coming to join us. We were an eclectic mix of Indians and foreigners, mainly an older crowd who were all eager to claim the chairs that were placed in a circle around a shallow, open pit, where younger and more flexible members of the audience could sit on cushions.

Nochur would deliver his discourse, with the aid of microphones, from a seat on the far side of the pit.

An Indian man was gently pushing his way through the

     Subhuti Anand Waight

waiting throng. I started to resist, but then the Westerner beside me murmured, "He has the door key." I relaxed my defensive stance to let him by. This was it. The door was unlocked and opened.

Trying not to look and act like mad shoppers at a Black Friday sale, when department stores throw open their doors to the mob, we pressed through the entrance. Old ladies took no precedence. It was every meditator for himself. I walked quickly to the left, as advised by friends who'd been there before.

To my dismay, the few people ahead of me had thrown bags and scarves over their neighbouring chairs, reserving them for friends. So, in the area where I wanted to sit, all front row seats were booked.

I had to act fast. More people were coming behind me and claiming chairs in the second row. Instinctively, I grabbed a vacant chair and dragged it into the front row, extending the line by one more seat, and sat down.

I was expecting to hear an objection, since I'd obviously disturbed someone's idea of how to organize this audience, but nobody seemed to mind. In fact, the idea caught on and more and more people brought chairs to the front, so eventually there was an extended front row, going all the way around the central pit back to the entrance.

Dark looks and muttered curses greeted some of those who'd shamelessly reserved two or three front row seats, as new arrivals observed the situation and reluctantly filled up the rows behind. But, as a single meditator, having made no reservations, I was free from blame.

When we were all in, an elderly, distressed-looking lady approached a friend next to me and, almost in tears, exclaimed, "I swear I am never going to keep a seat for anyone again. It's just too much stress!"

As for myself, I felt I needed a front row seat, not because I imagined it would bestow added spiritual blessings upon me, but simply to be able to see Nochur clearly and absorb the whole picture – the man, the library and the crowd. Also, I knew it would help to keep me alert. Hiding in a second or third row, I'd be more tempted to nod off or space out.

Once I was sure of my seat, I left my bag on it and strolled outside into the morning sunshine. For some reason, or maybe none at all, I felt infused by a light, happy feeling.

Suddenly, inexplicably and probably temporarily, I belonged here. I was at home. This part of the ashram was lovely, located far from the traffic noise on the streets, with the slopes of Mount Arunachala embracing us closely from behind.

I was enjoying it all. And, for today, at least, the stress of the waiting game was over. Tomorrow, the same thing would be happening at another location because the news had spread that Mooji had changed his mind and would be giving satsang for six days in Tiru before leaving for Rishikesh. I simply had to check him out.

The big hitters were coming to town and opening for business. Typically, Satsang-givers in Tiru attract audiences ranging from five to fifty people. Nochur had pushed that up to 500. Mooji would take it even higher and then Amma, the amazing hugging phenomenon, would take it through the roof.

They are all on my spiritual bucket list. Not that any of it is likely to make me more enlightened. I could probably be as blissful having a cup of chai on the street.

But still…. There's something in it. I just don't know what to call it. Nochur calls it Atman, the Supreme Self. Even with all our human failings, including the need for front row seats, we are drawn here because of it. Somehow, we can feel it is just that little bit closer, here near Ramana's mountain.

After Nochur's lecture had ended, I realized, after a while, that I couldn't remember a single thing he'd said. That certainly wasn't true for every member of his audience. For

　　　　Subhuti Anand Waight

example, Atmanand, a well-known Dutch scholar of Sanskrit and Buddhist texts, who will soon be giving Satsang himself, was happily taking notes throughout Nochur's discourse.

You could tell, just by looking at him, that he was in heaven in such academic company. But me? I had bathed in the inner bliss, the pool of energy that had softly and silently filled the hall, spreading over us and within us.

It helped me understand that I was no longer interested in spiritual concepts and scriptural explanations. I'd had my fill of that, years ago. No, I was here for the vibe, for the taste of meditation, for the quieting of my mind as it listened to Nochur's spiritual lullaby, thereby – at least for a short while – forgetting itself.

SATSANG WITH MOOJI

"Are you going to Mooji so early?"

The questioner was my neighbour. We were chatting over our breakfast porridge in a small café, close to where we lived. It was eight o'clock in the morning. The banana porridge had been recommended to me and was tasty, but for sheer quantity and speed of delivery, the German Bakery porridge was the clear Tiru prize winner.

"Well, I'm an early bird," I replied. "I can either wait in my room or wait outside the rice mill, so I may as well go there now."

She promised to join me later. I paid my modest bill, then walked for about 20 minutes to the Vetri Rice Mill, whose name reflected its agricultural past, but which now served as a Satsang venue.

Of course, I was not the first. About twenty people had already formed a line ahead of me, on the road outside the property. But it was an easy wait, because everyone was in a good mood, excited about Mooji's Satsang.

The young woman next to me was Hungarian, visiting India for just two weeks.

"First time with Mooji?" I inquired.

She nodded. "And you?"

"Well, I accidentally met him in the street, but this is the first Satsang," I replied.

The morning was sunny and refreshingly cool. We were standing in the shade of the mill wall and, on the other side of the road, open fields offered a fabulous view of Mont Arunachala. People were arriving in rickshaws, on bicycles, and on foot. The line kept snaking backwards, but I already knew our line was meaningless because I'd been warned that a lottery system was waiting for us inside.

At nine o'clock, we filed in, dropped off our bags and shoes, then sat in about a dozen lines outside the Satsang hall, one behind each other. A few minutes later, the person sitting at the head of each line was invited to pull a number out of a hat. Whoever pulled "1" could take their line into the hall first, and so on.

My line leader pulled "3," which was fortunate enough, and even though I could have enjoyed a close seat on the floor, I prudently opted for a nice, comfortable, plastic chair about half-way back on the right side of the hall.

My ageing knees whispered, "Thank you, Subhuti."

Mooji's advance team had, I'd been told, done a fabulous job in cleaning up the old mill which hadn't been used for a number of years. The walls looked white and freshly painted, the floor was covered with rush matting and there were photos of enlightened beings hanging from the rafters and pinned to the walls.

I recognized Ramana Maharshi, of course, and also noted

Anandamayi Ma, Ramakrishna, Nisargadatta Maharaj, Papaji… Even Jesus Christ and Satya Sai Baba made an appearance.

The ushers were quietly efficient, somehow fitting over 600 people into the space. Incense was carried around in a burner and offered for inhaling. Music played softly. The lighting was pleasant.

Mooji came in around 10:15 am and sat in a cane chair on a platform in the front of the hall. He was fitted with a radio mike, then sat silently with us for a few minutes before opening up the meeting for questions.

I didn't pay much attention to the first question. As I recall, a young French woman said she was troubled by an inability to focus on daily tasks after diving deeply into meditation. Rather than listening to Mooji's response, I was being seduced by a growing sense of inner space. Having closed my eyes, I was sinking into the energy of silence, presence and emptiness.

It was the same space I'd experienced with Nochur, the Brahmin scholar, also with other Satsang givers in Tiru, as well as on the mountain in Ramana's caves. It didn't seem to matter what the outer structure happened to be. As soon as the surroundings were quiet, and one's attention was focusing inward, the quality of meditation was always ready to manifest.

To give one example: my favourite Satsang took place every morning at ten o'clock in an unassuming-looking house on ShivaShakti Road, not far from Ramana's ashram. We'd all gather by 9:30 and wait. Then a little old Indian lady, wrapped in a pink sari and shawl, would come down the outside stairway, obviously with some physical difficulty, and walk slowly into the room.

She came like a ball of silence, filling the room with energy. She said nothing. She sat on a chair for about two minutes. Then she got up and, taking her time, turning

                    Subhuti Anand Waight

slowly, she looked with half-closed eyes at each one of us. Her silence filled with room with meditation.

Then she slowly walked out and, again with difficulty, slowly climbed the stairs. End of Satsang. I heard tales that, once a year, this woman spoke, but some Westerners who'd been there expressed disappointment at her verbal communication.

Mooji, however, was about to demonstrate his talent for bringing people into the same experience through words. A Russian woman, accompanied by a translator, came to the microphone and asked, "I want to know it now. I don't want to wait."

Mooji accepted the challenge and talked her into an awareness of…well…what he calls "The Self." Taking his time and making sure the woman understood, he asked her first to drop any preoccupation with the past. Then, when she was ready, he asked her to do the same thing with the future. Then, unexpectedly, with the present as well.

Dropping the present? Yes, in the sense that the woman had any distractions concerning other people in the room, etc. Then he asked her to cast aside any impressions of the body and the mind.

This went on, until finally all that was left to experience was a state of pure presence or awareness, without any input, thoughts or feelings. He then invited her to recognize this awareness as her true Self.

The way he did it, the whole room – those who wanted to anyway – could travel with him, each of us arriving at his or her own inner core of consciousness.

"Come along with us, it's a free ride," he joked to the audience, as he talked the Russian woman through the experience.

It may sound too easy to be true, but that's because of the limitation of my language. Mooji did a good job. I've met very few people who can give others a taste of meditation by talking them into it, and he now joined this select band.

However, perhaps I should add a word of caution: in my view, he gave the woman a taste of something which, in order to become a permanent state, would require a much deeper form of self-inquiry. It was an introduction, not a one-way ticket to enlightenment. But she seemed happy enough with what had transpired and thanked Mooji before sitting down.

Satsang lasted for two hours. There were a couple of surprises.

A tall, white-bearded Westerner, half naked and dressed only in a lunghi, came to the microphone to sing a song of gratitude.

A young Indian guy almost jumped across the room in his enthusiasm to recite a poem about nonduality, listing opposites such as light and dark, life and death, but after each pairing repeating, "It's the same."

Mooji took it all in good heart. Then it was time to go. He will be giving Satsang for another five days. I don't know if I'll go again, but for sure it was a gift to be at this one.

By the way, in case you're wondering, I'm not here in Tiru looking for new spiritual guides. No, it's more like an interest in widening my perspective; an understanding that, as the Buddha once said, you can taste the ocean from anywhere and it has the same salty taste.

There seems to be a good supply of salt here in Tiru.

     Subhuti Anand Waight

THE MUDDY PATHS TO INNER SILENCE

"Oh no, it's raining!"

It was still dark when I poked my head out of the sliding glass window of my hotel room and listened. Sure enough, I could hear the sound of raindrops softly and steadily pattering on the leaves of the trees opposite my balcony.

Dawn followed soon afterwards, revealing a murky, grey, cloudy sky. No sign of a blue patch anywhere. This was bad news. I had come from Tiru to Auroville for only one reason: to experience the atmosphere inside the golden globe of the Matrimandir.

Entry to this elusive, protected space is tricky, because if you're a newcomer, never having visited before, you can't book tickets in advance. You have to come in person to Auroville's Visitors Centre and there you can get a ticket for entry in one or two days' time.

I'd left Tiru early on Wednesday morning, on a seven o'clock bus, had been dropped on the main highway, then hitch-hiked to Auroville, first in a car, then on the back of a motorbike.

Hitching rides is easy in Auroville, I discovered, even with a suitcase. People are friendly, especially in helping you get around. After a quick detour for a morning coffee, I went to the booking office and got a ticket for the earliest available time-slot: Saturday morning at 08:45.

But there, on the bright yellow ticket, was the warning:

"IN CASE OF RAIN, or if the pathways and Garden areas are too muddy, the Park of Unity is closed and all appointments of the day are cancelled."

Since tickets are free, there's no customer leverage and no arguing about it.

Viewing the Matrimandir from outside required no advance booking and happened on a clear, bright Thursday morning. The golden orb glittered in the brilliant sunshine. But Saturday morning was wet and incredibly humid. It felt like, any moment, I could be drenched in a torrential downpour.

Leaving my hotel, I met a French couple on the road, also heading for the Mandir. The rain seemed to be lightening up, but it was still wet enough to dampen my clothes. We got a ride to the Visitors Centre, where, at the appointed time, we were issued with blue passes, and then shown a video about the conceptual vision of Auroville. My eyes were looking at the story on the screen, but my mind was thinking, "How muddy are the paths to the Mandir?"

We walked to the buses. The earth was wet, but not flooded. The rain held off, but the sky looked threatening. We were driven to a holding area, within sight of the golden globe, which sat tantalizingly close, floating amid a sea of green lawns.

How near and yet so far!

We were told to sit and wait, while a nice old gentleman told us how to behave once inside the dome. Then we had to wait some more because we were deemed to be too early.

I looked at the clouds, massing above us. Was that a raindrop on my head?

At last, we were picked up by a guide and invited to walk towards our destination. But then, half-way, our guide took us on an elaborate detour through the gardens and around an amphitheatre.

Finally, we arrived, slipped out of our shoes and walked silently, in single file, through one of twelve lotus petals surrounding the base of the globe. We then descended beneath the globe itself and were invited to sit silently around a circular, white marble fountain with a crystal ball in the middle. It was lovely, but still, it was outside. Surely now, even if the clouds burst asunder, we'd be allowed in?

At last, the moment arrived.

We were led silently up a narrow stone staircase, into a softly lit, circular anteroom, where we all put on a pair of clean white socks – white marble needs to be protected from sweaty feet.

We filed through a door and began a long, slow climb up a circular white ramp with white handrails, winding its way up and around the inner wall of the dome.

I loved this part of the journey. It was like something out of *Star Trek* or *Close Encounters* or *Star Wars*. We were leaving Planet Earth, ascending to the realm of the gods.

For the first time since waking up in my hotel room, I became fully present and stopped worrying. We were safe. We were inside. It could rain cats and dogs. Nothing could stop us.

We passed through a massive archway, kept ascending, and emerged at last into a huge, white, circular auditorium.

It was stunningly beautiful.

You could feel the silence.

We walked slowly, softly and silently to our seats: small white, square cushions, placed around the periphery of the chamber.

I sat down, awed by my aesthetic surroundings. There were twelve columns supporting the space. The lighting was kept dim and misty, like some Ancient Greek temple at dawn.

In the centre of the circular space before us was a large crystal sphere, lit by a shaft of light from the top of the dome.

I was impressed at how silent our group could be. Fifty people, coming from around the world, some of them just curious rather than experienced meditators. And we all sat in deep silence.

Or maybe the silence of the chamber sat inside us.

One or two people coughed, but surprisingly few for such a big company. If somebody coughed too loudly, an usher silently approached and guided them out. We who remained, opened our hearts and souls, bathing in the beauty and in the silence.

Truth to tell, I'd not been much interested in Sri Aurobindo, the mystic who'd inspired Auroville, nor in The Mother, his spiritual companion, who'd given the vision for the Matrimandir.

I wasn't much interested in the community, its purpose, its ideals. But, oh yes, I was impressed by their creation of this silence. This was the core of it all, just as it is the core of every spiritual experience.

This was the source itself, provoked by this fabulous environment which mirrored the silent temple within us all. A reminder, or perhaps more like a revelation, that whenever we find a good excuse to stop thinking, we discover we are the consciousness that is always there behind the mind.

We sat for twenty minutes, then a gong sounded and we slowly rose and filed out.

Soon, I was in a taxi, leaving Auroville behind, heading back to Tiru.

     Subhuti Anand Waight

The clouds suddenly burst open and it poured heavily with rain the whole way back.

I didn't mind.

THE HUGGING SUPERSTAR

"The bus we are providing is free. There is no charge whatsoever."

The owner of this local travel company, located just opposite the Ramana ashram, is proud of his generosity. Of course, he is hoping for our business in other ways – flight and train tickets, perhaps, or foreign exchange – but this coach trip to see Amma, the hugging saint, is free for us Western pilgrims.

We climb aboard and soon we are off, threading our way through Tiru's busy streets. It's a short ride, no more

 Subhuti Anand Waight

than 12 kilometers, but, for me, it contains the surprise of the evening.

"Subhuti?"

I turn and look into the eyes of a German woman, about my age, one row back. She has silver hair, blue eyes, a pleasant-looking face. Nothing clicks in my memory.

"It's Darshan," she says and smiles.

Then I remember. We were lovers, way back in 1974 in London, when I was a meditation teacher and then again, in 1976, when she had just returned from Pune wearing orange clothes and a mala.

OMG. How extraordinary. To meet like this, out of the blue. Neither of us can quite believe it.

The bus arrives and we're getting out. She needs to wait for a friend, so we make a date for the following day: 4pm at the German Bakery. Then she disappears in the crowd. And what a crowd.

A meeting with Amma offers one major difference to my experiences with other spiritual teachers, gurus and Satsang-givers in Tiru. Amma has mass appeal. She's not just for meditators. She's nothing less than a living saint, and thousands of people from every level of Indian society want to be blessed by her embrace.

I was expecting an indoor hall, but it's a huge, open space, bigger than a football pitch, filled with countless rows of plastic chairs, fenced in, all the way around, by a ten-foot high wall of brightly coloured cotton cloth.

Following the crowd, I make my way forward. A friendly official directs me to a side booth for visitors from abroad. Having had my nationality noted and having explained that I'm a first-timer with Amma – very important this – I'm escorted towards the stage and given a seat with other Westerners about twenty rows from the front.

I already know that, at some stage during the evening, tokens will be issued to us with letters from 'A' thru 'Z,' informing us when our turn will come to join the line for Amma's hug.

The sun is still bright but is setting swiftly and soon sinks behind the cloth wall. A short while later, the tiniest sliver of a new moon appears amid the gathering dusk.

Amma arrives at around 6:15, shadowed by a purple and gold umbrella, and the stage is filled with dignitaries from around the state of Tamil Nadu. This, I soon understand, is going to be a tedious delaying factor. We have to sit through almost two hours of speeches, as every political and spiritual leader in the state pays homage to her.

I find myself wishing I'd met her in Germany, or some other country, but I'm not going to quit now.

The speeches are followed by Amma's laudable views on the need to protect Mother Nature and Planet Earth from man's destructive ways. Her warning words are read aloud by a man sitting next to her, while her message is illustrated by images of whales and honeybees on a huge video screen at the back of the platform.

Prayers follow, also spelled out on the screen, and we are reminded, perhaps a little too repetitively, of human weaknesses, such as seeking outer wealth rather than inner peace of mind.

Bhajan singing comes as a welcome relief. Amma herself leads the singing, beating time with a stick or lightly flicking her finger-cymbals. Now the crowd is singing along with the musicians onstage.

Tokens are handed out. Naturally, I'm hoping for 'A1,' but, alas, I am handed 'W5.'

"Don't worry, it's a good token," assured the young Western man who pressed the token into my palm. Seeing my disappointment, he adds, "It'll be after midnight, but you're a first-timer, so you get priority."

Staring at the number in my hand, I reflect that 'priority' is, indeed, a relative term. Oh well.

     Subhuti Anand Waight

Hugging starts at 9:15 and we all know that Amma won't stop now until the whole crowd has been embraced, every last one of us, one by one. In this respect, she is truly an awesome phenomenon, sometimes sitting for 12 or 14 hours without a break until everyone has been hugged.

Now that I have my token, I am free to walk around and soon I'm rubbing shoulders with other people I know from the Tiru Satsang scene.

One Swedish friend got lucky. She was about to give up and go home, when a passing official gave her a 'G' token. She's a mother with child, which, apparently gives her even higher priority than first timers like me.

Rumours that people from abroad get preferential treatment over Indians prove untrue. Watching local people join the lines on either side of the platform leading up to Amma, I have to concede this is fair, if a little annoying.

A rotating board in the centre of the crowd announces the letters now being invited to join the lines. I'm happy to note we get from 'A1' to 'C5' fairly quickly, but then everything slows down…and slows down….

Around midnight, feeling peckish, I slip through the curtain wall to enjoy food being offered freely as *prasad* at a large booth with huge cooking pots behind the counter. Not many people are queuing, but as I approach, a number of poor-looking, local children race past me and fight and wriggle their way to the front.

I'm touched, and slightly shocked by their desperation. Also, by their skill and professionalism. This isn't a one-off race for food. This is their way of life.

I'm not that hungry – I've never been that hungry in my life – so I turn away and decide to join a nearby line for free chai instead.

Instantly, the man behind the counter hands me a tray with a dozen cups, all filled with chai, and it seems that now I've become a waiter, offering chai to others, which is unexpected and fun. But I do remember to keep one for myself.

An hour later, I check the food lines and they're completely empty. I stroll over and receive a paper plate with a hot dollop of grain-like substance and, like everyone else, start eating it with my fingers.

To my surprise and delight, it tastes delicious. I can't get enough of it.

"What is this called?" I ask a nearby group of men, pointing to my plate.

"Suji…subji…upma…kidgerie…." Many names are offered, but I sense I'm missing the one I'm trying to remember from years gone by. I guess 'upma' comes closest.

But then, in a dawn of understanding, I realize it's true name. This is, indeed, prasad, a gift of love. Even afterwards, I couldn't figure out if the food really tasted that good or if it was Amma's nearby presence or my late-night state of consciousness.

Now, at last, the letters are dropping towards the tail end of the alphabet. We're down to 'T,' but there's a crowd control problem developing. The entrance to the line has been besieged by a big group of local Indian women, all of whom are holding 'Z' tokens, but they all want to be first in line when their number comes up.

Not wishing to miss 'W,' I join the throng and shuffle and squeeze my way to the mouth of line, where several harassed officials are trying to control admission through the barriers.

The guy in charge is ruthless, physically shoving people away, but there's no alternative. He has to do this if any kind of order is to be maintained. Unfortunately, I arrive in front of him while 'U' is still being shown on the central board, so I have become part of the problem.

"I'm afraid I'm going to miss my plane!" I explain, offering this lame excuse to justify my behaviour, but he isn't buying it.

        Subhuti Anand Waight

"Wait!" he commands, pushing me back.

At last, the magic letter 'W' appears on the board and I'm ushered through. It's certainly a relief to be out of the crush. I'm surprised there were no actual fights, but most people manage to maintain a happy mood, even when stressed. After all, the saint herself is in sight.

I pass through a bag check, but nobody seems interested in taking my little backpack and the people behind me in line are threatening to overtake me.

No way! I throw my bag over the barrier onto a red plastic chair and hope it'll be there when I come back. I don't want to stop now and, anyway, there's nothing in it except a sleeveless jacket.

The line moves steadily. Now we're approaching the stage itself, the lights are getting brighter, the music louder and the excitement is building.

I'm walking up a narrow sloping pathway towards where Amma is sitting.

My token has been checked half-a-dozen times and now I'm being greeted by cheerful, smiling, Western helpers who are telling me to wipe any sweat off my face, so as not to leave it on Amma when she hugs me.

"No shoes!" says one and I immediately kick off my expensive trainers which fall to the ground, out of sight somewhere beneath the stage. I may lose them, but I don't care. I can't stop now.

The stage surrounding Amma is brightly-lit and filled with people, mostly Westerners, who have already been hugged and who now want to sit quietly and watch. Everyone seems to be wearing white.

Amma is very close now, just a couple of hugs away. It's 2:15 in the morning and I'm wide awake and feeling suddenly elated, lifted by the glow of good vibes surrounding her.

There's one person ahead of me. I'm held gently by two helpers. One has the back of my head, the other my left arm.

"Nationality?" one of them asks.

"English," I reply.

The space opens up, the woman herself is right in front of me, sitting effortlessly cross-legged on her little platform. She is big, wide, and welcoming.

I'm gently pushed towards Amma. "English," a helper announces.

She takes me firmly in her arms and pulls my head down to her right shoulder, then presses her own head against mine. My eyes are closed. Everything is dark and warm and soft. Seconds seem like hours.

"Amore…amore…amore," Amma murmurs in my ear, but since I'm not Italian I can't say for sure that's what she was saying. Something like that.

Time's up. I am pulled away. I turn my back towards Amma and walk down a steep ramp to ground level. I feel light and start laughing. I feel like skipping, but the slope's too steep. Better not. I find my shoes beneath the stage, then pick up my bag.

I could have sat on the stage, but enough is enough. I'm ready to go.

Heading out through the stadium, which by now is half-empty, I run into a group of young Chinese women. They smile at me.

"Have you been hugged?" I ask them.

"Yes!" they reply, nodding happily, and we all burst into laughter. We enjoy sharing this moment of understanding. No words are needed.

There are no buses back to Tiru, but plenty of rickshaw drivers are waiting patiently, hoping to make an early morning killing.

"Five hundred rupees," says one.

Without too much effort, I get him down to three hundred. Then I find a young German woman who lives near me and is willing to share the cost. This makes the ride affordable and, given the early hour, quite reasonable.

We climb in. We chat about Amma all the way home. I take a long, hot shower and by the time I switch out the light it's 3:30 am. By 9:30, I'm awake, sit up in bed and start writing.

As I finish this little story, I'm astonished to find that I am weeping. I don't know why, but tears of joy are running down my face. I feel helpless, hopeless… and blessed by I don't know what. Call it divine grace.

I find myself standing naked under the shower, but I haven't turned on the taps because it feels like I'm bathing in light. I feel tension in my poor shoulders and suddenly see how they have been trying, all my life, in their own unconscious way, to raise me up to this blissful state.

How unnecessary, when all the time, this grace has been waiting to shower down upon me.

India is a strange and wonderful place.

The thought 'Who Am I?' will destroy all other thoughts,
and like the stick used for stirring the burning pyre,
it will itself in the end get destroyed. Then,
there will arise Self-Realization

~ Sri Ramana Maharshi.

Ramana Maharshi

Amma

Atmananda

Sharada

Mooji

Siva Sakthi

Yogi Ram

ONCE UPON A TIME IN INDIA

"How come you know so many people here?"

The young Canadian guy who was drinking chai with me seemed puzzled. I'd told him I'm a first timer in Tiru, recently arrived, yet here I was, saying 'Hello' to people – first in the ashram, then around the chai shop – like we were old friends.

Two women, both dressed in white saris, had greeted me with surprise and enthusiasm. Two men had said 'Hi' in a similarly friendly fashion.

"It's a long story," I told the Canadian. He was about 25 years old, tall, athletic looking, with a mop of dark brown hair. We'd seen each other a couple of times in the ashram and had struck up a conversation while standing outside the ashram's main hall during the evening Vedic chanting.

He was, as I recall, fresh out of university – in Toronto, I believe – and on an extended tour of the East. He'd come to Tiru from Nepal a few days earlier.

"I've got time to hear it," he answered, with a grin. To emphasize the point, he pulled up another chair to rest his feet, dragged his backpack a little closer and looked at me expectantly. He wasn't going to let me off the hook.

"Okay. Well, one of those women was in a notorious German movie, called *Ashram in Poona*, back in the Seventies, which showed naked people screaming and fighting with each other. It caused quite a stir," I told him.

"The other was a 'chai mama' at a big commune in Oregon, in the Eighties. She was driving a pickup truck to bring tea and snacks to our work crews," I continued. "One of those guys was a cop, toting a gun, on the Ranch. The other was a mechanic who was good at repairing giant bulldozers."

"Interesting," commented the Canadian. "So, if you've known each other all these years, how come you're surprised to see each other?"

"Okay, like I say, it's a bit of a tale." I bought us both another chai, leaned back in my chair, smiled and began: "Once upon a time, in India, a long time ago…"

I told him about a charismatic enlightened mystic, then called Bhagwan Shree Rajneesh, now known as Osho, who in 1974 created an ashram in Pune near Mumbai. It was a high energy place that attracted thousands of people, and by the beginning of the Eighties had become so overcrowded that a new, bigger ashram was urgently needed.

"That's when we all pulled up stakes and went to America," I explained. "That's when we built a town for 3,500 people on a deserted cattle ranch in Oregon."

"Yes, I know about that," commented my young friend. "I saw some of that Netflix series."

"*Wild Wild Country*," I reminded him. "Good, that saves me a long explanation!"

"After Osho was kicked out of America in 1985, the Ranch collapsed," I went on. "Osho went around the world trying to start a new commune, but no one wanted him.

In the end he returned to Pune and died there in 1990."

Then I explained how the community of 'sannyasins' – as Osho's disciples are called – who had been living with Osho in Pune began to break up.

"Some of those people wanted to be with a living spiritual teacher," I explained. "Quite a lot of them ended up in Lucknow with a guy called Poonja, or Papaji as he became known. He was about eighty years old at the time, and had been with Ramana Maharshi, so he was teaching Advaita and the search for the Self."

"Did you go?" asked my Canadian companion.

I laughed. "No! I was upset by the drift to Papaji," I recalled. "I was determined that Osho would be my only spiritual guide. I used to say to people: 'I'm sexually polygamous but spiritually monogamous.' So, I was very judgmental about it."

I went on to explain that Papaji was attracting other Western followers, not just Osho disciples, since he'd been mentioned by a French monk, Henri Le Saux, who'd written several books on *advaita* and who'd become a Hindu sannyasin himself.

In this way, Papaji drew people to Lucknow who today are well-known spiritual teachers themselves, including Mooji, Gangaji, Andrew Cohen and others.

"What irritated me was that Papaji sanctioned dozens of his followers to go out into the world and give Satsang, and some of them were complete idiots, suffering from what I diagnosed as PSE." I said, still feeling some of my old, self-righteous indignation.

"PSE?"

I laughed at the memory. "Premature spiritual ejaculation," I explained. "But it was a confusing paradox. I wanted to dismiss Papaji as a fraud, but in all honesty I could not. Friends of mine have told me, very sincerely, that they didn't begin to go deep into self-inquiry and the spiritual search until they met him.

"Anyway, Papaji died in 1997 and the scene in Lucknow broke up. Those who wanted to continue to explore advaita decided to come to Tiru, to the source, here at Ramana's ashram."

I added that not all my old friends had come to Tiru via Papaji. For example, there were people who had been with Ramesh Balsekar in Mumbai, another advaita teacher.

"So, here you all are," reflected the Canadian. He took another sip of his chai, looked at me and asked, "Are you still with Osho?"

"Yes, but I'm not as arrogant and exclusive as I used to be," I reflected.

His next question made me laugh.

"Do you ever want to give Satsang yourself. I mean, you're pretty experienced."

"It would be fun, I imagine, but probably a distraction from my own process. And then you have to listen to all those questions and come up with advice and suggestions."

"What about Mooji?"

"What about him?"

"Is he the real thing?"

"Good question. I don't know. He's got some beautiful qualities. He seems very open to people, he welcomes them, he receives them and makes them feel heard and understood. I think his guidance does help people. And for sure he's got a big heart."

"And?"

"I don't feel he's awakened in the same sense as Ramana and Osho were. But the bottom line is, I really won't know for sure until I'm awakened myself."

"When will that be, do you think?"

I looked past him at an old poster for a Mooji Satsang, stuck on a railing. It said: "Enough seeking...now find!"

"Any moment now," I answered.

THE SATSANG SCENE

Sharada seems to be an ordinary, pleasant-looking Indian woman of about fifty years old. There's nothing remarkable about her. She stays in a nice house on the far side of Mount Arunachala, about halfway round the girivalam, the holy walk that takes pilgrims around the mountain.

Sharada's Satsang room has a white marble floor and the walls and ceiling are painted white. The plastic chairs are white. Obviously, she likes white, so with my white shirt I'm in tune. Everything looks clean and new and the bathroom is Western standard – and white.

Looking out through the wall-to-ceiling windows, the towering shape of Arunachala is seen close by. It's a nice setting for a morning Satsang, offered by a middle-aged woman wearing an elegant sari who apparently spends most of her time in San Diego, California.

When she answers questions, Sharada's answers are intelligent but unsurprising. Her views are classical advaita, focusing on the one true Self that pervades all things, hidden from us because of our identification with the ego-self. Surrender the ego-self and the true Self immediately becomes manifest.

So far, so good…and so what? Any advaita teacher can tell the same spiritual story.

It is when we move into the energy transmission phase of Sharada's Satsang that the ordinary starts to become remarkable. With eyes closed, I sense that I am beginning to be bathed in a soft, sensual, healing power or force, rather like slipping into a warm spiritual bath.

This lovely energy field, suffused with white light, surrounds me and is slowly intensifying, so that my sense of being a physical body becomes less and less distinct. Within this field, it is easy for the mind to slow down and cease generating thoughts. Thoughts do come, but only once in a while.

The energy does not seem to be emanating from Sharada herself. It just seems to happen, although, obviously, she must be the catalyst.

This delightful experience goes on for about an hour, then she brings us back. Within a few minutes, Satsang is over and we are filing out of the room into the morning sunshine, looking for a rickshaw to take us back to town.

Also out here, on this side of the mountain, Werner, the old German hippie, gives Satsang twice a week. He has the advantage of a truly wonderful rural location, way out in the fields, far from the noisy traffic.

Satsang is held on top of his house, under a shady roof of thatched coconut leaves, accompanied by birdsong and the occasional mournful "moo" from a local cow.

I can't listen to Werner for long without spacing out. Maybe it's because he doesn't use a microphone or because he rambles or because his answers and advice are mostly predictable common sense. But Werner has a certain joy in his eyes and a humour to his responses that makes him lovable and enjoyable to be with.

It's relaxing to sit with him on his roof, especially when he tells tales of his time with Amma, with whom he fell in love way back in 1981. She gave him such a hard time, apparently, that he had no choice but to awaken to the Self.

Werner sits cross-legged on the floor the whole time and keeps with him a pet dog who rests peacefully by his side. His Satsangs begin and end with a silent meditation.

Swami Atmananda is a very different kettle of fish. I have already experienced his meetings up in Rishikesh, where he normally resides. He's a nice guy, a learned Dutch scholar, and very sincere in his efforts to explain the sacred scriptures of various faiths.

Since his Satsang is here in town, on the roof of the house near where I'm staying, it's easy to stroll over and listen to him.

The energy in his Satsang is pleasant, but he's really not my cup of tea. He's too intellectual. Understanding the meaning of scriptures, as he does, isn't the same as experiencing what they're talking about.

Inevitably, I can't stay long. One of the beauties of the Satsang circuit here in Tiru is that you don't have to stay until the event is over. You can slip out whenever you like. Another plus is that all of them are free.

Intensive retreats, usually held elsewhere, after the Tiru season is over, do cost serious money. But these Satsang events are without charge.

Maharishikaa Preeti gives Satsang right next door to Ramana's ashram. She seems younger than Sharada, lives in Mumbai, answers questions for three hours, drinks a lot of tea during this time, and is very clear and definite in expressing her ideas about spiritual development.

                    Subhuti Anand Waight

For me, that's a bit of a problem. I learned a long time ago that being clear and definite may impress people who are confused and seeking certainty in their lives, but that doesn't mean that what is being conveyed is either true or profound.

I have to say, on the plus side, that Rishikaa handles interruptions well:

A dark-skinned sadhu with heaps of matted hair, naked except for a short lunghi tied around his waist, stalks proudly into one of her talks and stands right in front of her, blocking her view to the audience.

She pauses, and as he stares at her she raises one hand in silent greeting. The sadhu waves his stick in the air, looks at us with scorn as if we are mere spiritual amateurs, then strides out. Rishikaa continues where she'd left off.

Her main teaching, as far as I can tell, is that enlightenment needs to happen in the body – not on some ethereal plane – and needs to be integrated into daily life. Well, that makes sense. But, teachings aside, I found her energy field relatively weak compared with my experience of other Satsang givers.

I guess this makes me an energy junkie rather than a seeker of profound spiritual knowledge. Satsang energy brings with it a sense of inner expansion, dissolving boundaries and silencing mental chatter. It carries us beyond the little 'me' and gives a taste of the infinite Self.

Nochur, the eloquent Brahmin scholar, has completed his series of six talks, given in English. What a pity. I enjoyed him very much. He doesn't have disciples. He is a teacher, although he clearly embodies what he preaches and, intentionally or unintentionally, is also able to generate a strong energy field while speaking.

Mooji will soon leave for Rishikesh, after paying his respects to Amma which he did during her massive, one-night-only Satsang event. Mooji went out of his way to see her. I'm not sure if they hugged or just held hands, but I'm quite sure he didn't have to wait eight hours for his face-to-face connection as I did.

Oh, by the way, did I say the wait was worth it? Of course, I did.

I have already talked about the little old Indian lady called Sivasakthi Ma. For sheer simplicity and power, her 15-minute Satsang is a hard act to beat.

I visited a couple more Satsang-givers but I don't really think they're worth talking about, although they were pleasant enough. One talked about mindfulness, the other about peace of mind.

Peace of mind? That made me smile. I remember a wise spiritual teacher saying that you can have peace or you can have mind, but you can't have both together!

By the way, I know it's a totally different ballgame, but I would include Ayurvedic Massage as a Satsang experience – at least in some ways. For example, my Danish friends strongly recommended that I book a session with Rahul (not his real name because he doesn't need my promotion).

While it was happening, it didn't seem like much. Rahul obviously knew what he was doing and used a kind of rhythmic massaging motion, gently rocking my body as he squeezed and kneaded the muscles.

Afterwards, as I stood up, I nearly fell over.

"Careful!" he said.

I paid and left. Walking down the street, I felt very different. All my muscles had somehow become strangers to me. To the casual observer, it probably seemed that I was walking in a natural manner, at regular speed, but inside it felt like I was doing a Michael Jackson moon walk, as if I was watching the whole muscular-skeletal system in action, moving along, all by itself.

It left me wondering about Rahul. With a massage that seemed so ordinary, how did he manage to do that?

All Satsang-givers, it seems to me, have something to offer,

		Subhuti Anand Waight

partly, I suspect, because they occur within the energy field of Mount Arunachala itself. This mountain is something. It's hard to believe that a lump of rock can generate a buddhafield, but as far as I can see, that's exactly the case. Ramana himself, as is well known, was pulled to it and stayed here his whole life.

As for these modern teachers and their teachings, they all point in roughly the same direction: turn your attention from the outside world and focus on your inner reality.

But there's an attitude, shared by many advaita proponents, which holds that no effort is needed in spiritual development because all that is required is to recognize the true Self. When we understand that all is One, we've got it.

Too easy to be true? I'd say so. I liked Werner's objection to this spiritual shortcut: in one of his afternoon sessions, he pointed out that, unconsciously, we are all making tremendous effort to remain in the ego-self, mostly out of habit because it's all we know.

So, an intellectual recognition of the true Self, plus a brief experience of having a silent mind, isn't going to give us a permanent state of awakening. Old habits die hard and require a bit more effort to crack.

Good insight, Werner.

It's interesting to note that even though my own spiritual master, Osho, isn't part of the spiritual scenery here, and is rarely mentioned, his basic "method" – if you can call it that – of spiritual practice often shows up in what is being taught.

Osho's approach to meditation, like that of J. Krishnamurti and many other mystics – going back as far as Gautam Buddha himself – is to encourage people to become aware of their own thoughts and feelings, then learn to watch them, or 'witness' them, with indifference, without trying to either suppress them or judge them as good and bad.

Watching thoughts in this way robs them of energy,

creates distance from the thinking process, and slowly one learns to relax more and more into a deeper, more silent, more authentic, state of being. This approach, I find, has been widely accepted in Tiru.

So, those teachers who don't choose the illusory shortcut of immediate recognition of the Self tend, in one way or other, to offer witnessing as a way to gradually release oneself from the grip of the mind.

Not that this will guarantee your spiritual illumination. Enlightenment, so I am reliably informed, is not subject to ordinary cosmic laws, such as cause and effect, effort and result. You cannot 'do' it. But you can prepare the ground.

As the temperature starts to soar in Tiruvannamalai, the Satsang season comes towards its end, and teachers and gurus alike head north to Rishikesh or travel abroad.

Ramana's ashram and Mount Arunachala, of course, remain.

As one long term Tiru resident commented to me, "I'm not interested in Satsangs. All I need is the mountain."

That, at least, is never going to be a seasonal spiritual affair.

	Subhuti Anand Waight

MY DOCTOR'S JOURNEY

I am sick with a cold. I got it after sweating in a hot morning Satsang, then sitting almost naked under a rapidly whirling fan. The combination somehow disoriented my body's immune system and by next morning I was sick.

My cold developed into a cough. Almost immediately, the bug that was causing my runny nose also dived down into my chest and soon I was coughing up green mucous.

But fortune smiled at me. Every morning, an experienced, sympathetic German doctor came to visit me in my apartment, and nursed me back to health – completely free of charge.

How rare is that? Even in Germany, you wouldn't get this kind of home visit and personalized medical attention. And you certainly wouldn't get it for free when uninsured, like I was.

What was my secret? Well, as you may recall, I was travelling in a coach to see Amma, the hugging saint, when a woman behind me quietly asked, "Subhuti?"

It was my old friend Darshan whom I hadn't seen in years. We got together for a catchup gossip session and, among other things, she told me she had sold her medical practice in Berlin but still enjoyed practicing as a doctor.

It so happened that, in recent days, Darshan had been regularly attending the morning Satsangs of Atmananda, and, by chance, his lectures were taking place only a few houses from where I was staying.

So, it became a routine: Darshan would pop in to see me for a few minutes each morning, before joining the line to go up to the roof where Atmananda was talking.

"I want to see your mucous," she told me. An unusual, possibly even flirtatious, request from a female friend, but pretty standard for a doctor.

Obligingly, I coughed into a paper tissue. She peered at it closely, then commented, "Let's hold off on the antibiotics. I'll get you an expectorant cough medicine and meanwhile be sure to keep using your decongestant nose spray."

She'd already inspected the one I'd brought from Denmark and nodded her approval.

"It's important to keep your nose breathing openly, then your sinuses won't get infected," she advised.

When I pointed out that I'd already been using the spray for the recommended period, she assured me it was okay to continue, with no danger of damage to my nasal tissues.

"People get addicted to these sprays, that's why the limitation is there!" she said with a knowing smile. Hmm. Interesting things you get to know from doctors. It never occurred to me that the cleansing blast of a nasal spray could be an addictive experience.

On the last morning of Atmananda's series, Darshan

     Subhuti Anand Waight

came early and that's when I sat her down and said, "Okay, now tell me about your spiritual journey."

Darshan began by saying that soon after Osho died in 1990, she discovered that many of her friends were going to Lucknow to connect with Papaji.

"It wasn't so much that I wanted to see him," she reflected. "But I wanted to be with my friends and I was curious what they were up to." Thanks to one of those friends, she was able to stay in Papaji's house and experience his Satsangs from close-up.

"The energy was very strong and this was impressive," she recalled. "But I wasn't attracted to the teachings. Well, actually, he'd pretty much stopped teaching by that time and his daily Satsangs became a sort of circus.

"It seemed to me people were competing to get his attention and show how spiritually advanced they were, or how spiritually problematic!" she recalled with a chuckle.

Each winter for three years, Darshan visited Lucknow for a three-week period, then found herself more attracted to the Satsang scene in Mumbai. "I did go and see Ramesh Balsekar," she recalled. "But I was more attracted to Ranjit Maharaj."

This provoked my interest because I knew that Ranjit Maharaj had been a personal friend and contemporary of Nisargadatta Maharaj, the 'beedi baba,' so called because he ran a small beedi shop in Mumbai which was his sole source of income.

I'd heard Osho talk fondly about this 'beedi baba' in his discourses and, in the early Seventies, while still living in Mumbai himself, had apparently sent some of his sannyasins to see him.

There is a beautiful quote by Nisargadatta, which I think is quite well known, where he describes the basic transmission from his master:

"My Guru told me: Go back to that state of pure being, where the 'I am' is still in its state of purity before it got contaminated with 'I am this' or 'I am that.' Your burden is of false identifications – abandon them all."

But by the time Darshan became interested in visiting gurus in Mumbai, Nisargadatta was long gone, having left his body – as the saying goes – in 1981. Ranjit Maharaj was an old man by the time she met him.

"I really liked Ranjit," she told me. "The energy around him was light and delicate, and it was clear he was not interested in any kind of guru trip.

"He was a very sweet man, who felt that disciples would only be a burden to him. He would brush off any praise, saying it was all due to his lineage of teachers, including his own master, Siddharameshwar Maharaj."

When Ranjit died, Darshan lost interest in the Indian Satsang scene and focused on her work in Germany, while enjoying the meditative quiet of her remote holiday home in Greece.

Gradually, however, she became interested in an advaita teacher in Berlin called Karl Renz. He was the one who encouraged her to visit Tiru because he himself liked to spend long periods here each year.

"Is he still around?" I asked Darshan.

She laughed. "I had coffee with him yesterday in Da Mantra restaurant," she told me. "He's a farmer's son, very rebellious. He likes to shock people."

Before going, Darshan invited me to her birthday dinner party on the following Monday evening.

"How old are you?" I ventured. I'm never sure if I should ask this question of women, but I was guessing that Darshan wouldn't mind.

She looked at me mischievously, hesitated and said, "Well, let's put it this way: until Monday, I am still in my sixties!"

I looked at her in amazement and our eyes met, twinkling in laughter at the absurdity of the situation.

"So, you will be seventy? My god, I am 74!" I exclaimed.

                    Subhuti Anand Waight

"I can't believe it! When I tune into myself inside, I still feel like 17 years old."

After a moment, I added, "Until, of course, I look at my body, or start moving it around."

We both laughed, knowing how we were feeling in that moment: two teenagers locked in a time warp. Which left me with this question:

Who am I without my ageing body?

OUTSIDE THE GATES OF PARADISE

I'm not sure we're supposed to be here. We haven't been invited. The gate in front of us is shut. The people inside aren't coming out to say "Good morning" or even give us a silent namasté greeting.

But here we are. About twenty of us, making ourselves as comfortable as we can while settling down for an hour of silent meditation.

One guy, I think he's from Norway, sits as close to the gate as possible. He's been coming here for seven years just to meditate like this, with the couple inside. He didn't even know about the Ramana Ashram until after his arrival in Tiru.

A woman, I think she's French, has a room close by. But actually – so I'm told – sleeps on the ground just outside the gates every night to soak in the vibes.

I settle myself on a simple concrete bench a few metres

     Subhuti Anand Waight

from the gates, using a handy foam cushion to insulate my butt. The bench is in the shade, and on this warm sunny morning it offers a nice place to sit.

Others, with more flexible limbs and good postures, sit cross-legged on the ground, either directly in front of the gates or just to the side, with their backs against the wall. Everyone tries, as far as possible, to be in the shade.

Fortunately, this is a cul-de-sac. The house we're sitting outside of is at the end of a small, quiet road, about ten minutes' easy walking distance from Ramana's ashram. No traffic, no dogs, no beggars, no kids.

Before sitting down, I walk silently up to the gates and look inside. There is a low bungalow, quite large, surrounded by a lush garden, filled with trees, bushes and flowering shrubs. It looks like a well-tended, lovely garden paradise.

Now it's nine o'clock and time to sit. I close my eyes, lean back against the wall and relax. Almost immediately, I can sense the presence of a meditative energy field by now familiar to me and accessible in many places in Tiru.

Here, near this house, it seems particularly strong and welcoming. The gates may be shut, but the energy doesn't know it. We all sink gently into this silent space which deepens with the passing of time. This is what we came for, and this is what is available.

In a way, our situation reflects the strange karma of the 94 year-old mystic inside the bungalow. All his life, he has been seeking solitude. All his life, one way or another, he has been confronted with people's demand for his presence.

The mystic's name is Sri Lakshmana Swamy, and I learned about him through a book by author David Godman, titled *No Mind, I Am The Self*. It describes in detail the phases of Swamy's spiritual development and the challenges that went with it.

For example, as a reclusive hermit, living in a hut outside his village in Andhra Pradesh, he found that the more he tried to avoid people, the more he gained a reputation as a great yogi. His very desire not to be a guru, not to seek the praise and devotion of others, was seen as proof of his spiritual attainment.

Public demand became so intense that, on one occasion, fifty women encircled his small hut and together tried to lift the roof off in order to see him. When he opened the door to stop them, they rushed in and almost crushed him in a corner.

For a while, he was trapped, powerless to do anything. But then the women, seeing the problem, eventually arranged themselves in a line, and came to bow down before him, touch his feet, receive his blessing, and leave.

Later on, though, there were other problems. When his doctor advised him to move his body more, he started taking his dog for daily walks in the woods. But this was seen as far too mundane an occupation for a mystic.

Walking a dog? Anyone can do that! Local people became so hostile and angry with him, even driving herds of goats and sheep in his way to block his path, that he was forced to abandon the practice.

The biggest controversy in his life began at the age of 50, when he invited a 16 year-old girl called Sarada to come and live with him in his house. This enraged his mother, who until this time had been his caretaker and was also organizing any *darshans* or personal meetings that Swamy was allowing from time to time.

The mother became so jealous that she eventually turned against her own son and created many ugly rumours and difficulties for both Swamy and Sarada. Seen through the eyes of ordinary life, it was a classic mother-in-law situation!

Reading his life story, I couldn't help thinking Swamy could have used a good public relations manager which would have avoided many of his problems. As for his closeness to Sarada, one can only imagine the kind of uproar this would

                        Subhuti Anand Waight

have caused in the United States these days, with so much social sensitivity focusing on the exploitation of young women by powerful men.

But, in spite of the controversy, Swamy insisted that Sarada was a mature spiritual soul and that was why he wanted her close to him. In 1978, when she was nineteen, Swamy recognized that she had attained to a permanent state of thoughtlessness, residing in the Supreme Self, and declared her enlightenment.

The two mystics, Sarada and Swamy, have been together now for more than forty years. As I mentioned earlier, he is now 94, while Sarada is 61.

The book I was reading about them ended its story in 1985, so I can only conjecture what has happened since. At some point, no doubt, his troublesome mother died. At another point, they must have given up their small ashram in Andhra Pradesh and moved permanently to Tiru.

Perhaps I should have mentioned earlier that Swamy spent several years paying visits to Ramana Maharshi, staying in or near his ashram, absorbing his wisdom. So, it is natural that they should decide to retire in Tiru.

But, true to Swamy's spiritual style, they are not very accessible. For many years, both mystics have made it clear that they are not interested in meeting or talking with curious visitors or even with people who consider themselves to be meditators.

"There are very few people who are spiritually mature enough to benefit from the type of teaching that I offer," Swamy told his biographer David Godman.

As I understand it, this teaching consists of a powerful bond of trust, so the disciple can allow the guru, either Swamy or Sarada, to drive the ego-self out of his mind-body system, revealing the true Self as the sole remaining occupant.

As Sarada put it: "When you concentrate on God in the form of the Guru, he pulls you into himself and finally destroys you so completely that there is nothing left but God alone."

In recent years, a simple website invited seekers, who considered themselves sufficiently mature, to apply for a meeting with either Swamy or Sarada. Very few, so I hear, were granted access. The latest I hear is that this offer too has been closed.

The tall Norwegian told me that, a couple of years ago, Sarada used to come out from the bungalow and silently greet people on the other side of the gate. But this hasn't happened for a while.

What to do? Well, this small group of meditators isn't going to imitate the women who tried to lift the roof off Swamy's hut by rushing in and storming the bungalow. We're all far too polite for that and, anyway, it really does miss the point. The point, of course, is to focus on one's own meditation and inner silence. Inside or outside the gate, it's always the inner reality that counts.

Some activity does take place during our one-hour session. A European woman, aged about sixty, brings out trash for recycling, including a large, empty cardboard box with "amazon.in" on the side, and a whole bunch of empty plastic Bisleri drinking water bottles.

A local Indian woman on an electric-powered, three-wheeler recycling truck, arrives a few minutes later and takes it all away.

There's a European guy, maybe close to seventy, watering plants. When his tasks are completed for the day, he emerges through a side gate and walks quietly away. If he is the gardener, he's doing a great job.

Peacocks call to each other from various places in the garden, their shrill cries offsetting the silence of our meditation. A hawker on a bicycle, obviously selling something, calls from the far end of the street, but fortunately comes no closer.

One mobile phone goes off among the meditators, which,

     Subhuti Anand Waight

after some fairly desperate rummaging around inside a bag, is finally located and shut off. Well, naturally, it had to happen.

Half-way through the hour, I silently rise from my seat and take a couple of photos. I wonder if anyone will try to stop me, but nobody is even noticing.

There's no bell to announce the end of our session. It's really up to us to decide when our time is up. Some people stay on, but most of us, after about an hour, gather our things and silently walk away down the street.

Meditation over.

HOW TO GATECRASH SATSANG

Today, my Dutch friend Gayatri is my eyes and ears.

This morning, she guided me to the silent meditation outside the home of Swamy and Sarada. Now she calls me with her latest update.

"It's as I thought," she tells me. "Atmananda is sitting with Devaki and they're talking to a sizeable group of people."

"I'm coming!" I cry into my mobile and then, barefoot, walk briskly out of Ramana's ashram, snatching up my shoes on the way. No time to put them on.

I jump into a rickshaw and say "Ramsuratkumar Ashram!" Finally, I have learned how to pronounce this complex name, so the rickshaw drivers know what I'm talking about. We're off, swiftly slanting across the busy main road, turning left down the incredibly dusty Post Office Road, then a sharp right, then left, arriving within minutes at the ashram gates.

I already know the drill. I park my shoes in the little kiosk inside the gate and walk as quickly as possible past the main ashram building which is absolutely huge.

It has been built in the memory of Yogi Ramsuratkumar, a colourful character, a sort of spiritual hippie, who wandered all over India in search of truth, and whom thousands of people came to adore and recognize as an enlightened being.

He met Sri Aurobindo and Ramana Maharshi, but lived longer than either of these great mystics, eventually shedding his mortal coil in 2001. His main spiritual discipline was chanting mantras, especially those in honour of Rama.

Now it is one of his successors, Ma Devaki, who seems to be the main attraction, especially for Westerners. Devaki met the 'Divine Beggar,' as Yogi Ram was sometimes called, in 1986, while on a pilgrimage to Tiru when she was 34 years old.

Now in her late sixties, Devaki gives Satsang every evening at the ashram, around 7:15 pm, after the ritual chanting ends. I've been trying to see her on a couple of occasions, but alas, both times, Devaki announced she had other matters to attend to and left as soon as the chanting had finished.

Now, it seems, I will be lucky. Sure enough, at the end of this path, under a large white cloth canopy, Atmananda, the Dutch spiritual scholar, and Ma Devaki, devotee of the deceased guru, Yogi Ram, are sitting together.

Devaki is addressing the audience, which, I discover later, is made up exclusively of Atmananda's closest followers. Luckily, I don't get that. I think it's a public meeting and anyone can join. Good job I'm wearing my white shirt because all Atmananda's followers are wearing white.

Devaki speaks quite softly and listening from the back is difficult, especially when bells and chanting begin to seep out of the main ashram building. So, when some guy gets up from the front row and disappears, I naturally assume it's okay to walk down the side and slide into his vacant seat. Nobody stops me.

Gayatri, I notice, is sitting, relaxed and inconspicuous, about four rows back, on the far side of the audience. Unlike me, she's probably already guessed this is a private party.

It just so happens that the rooftop of her tiny apartment overlooks this ashram and so, earlier this afternoon, when she saw a group of Atmananda's disciples setting up this tent-like space, she put two and two together and correctly made five.

A short while later, Gayatri came inside the ashram gate to take a closer look and discovered that Atmananda and Devaki were already talking. That's when she called me.

Devaki is saying something interesting.

"You should not practice advaita in front of your guru," she tells the crowd.

Since both she and Atmananda have invited questions, I raise my hand. I still have no idea I'm not supposed to be here.

"What do you mean by that?" I ask, genuinely puzzled, but also worried that she may have already explained this exact point, just before I got here, which, of course, would make me look completely dumb.

But I do want to know because I thought advaita was the be-all and end-all of spirituality in Tiru. How can anyone not practice advaita, here in the advaita capital of the world?

"In advaita, if you focus your energy, you can begin to have the realization that I am the Self," Devaki explains, looking at me.

As I listen to her, I become suddenly aware that I'm wearing blue jeans, while everyone else in the front row is in white pants. Uh-oh.

Devaki doesn't seem to notice.

"This can create a certain attitude that, because you know the Self, you may begin to think that you no longer need your guru," Devaki continued.

"But this is an egoistic attitude," she added. "In front of

your guru, always see that the Self expresses through him and flows to you through his grace."

I get the point and thank her. She seems very at home in herself and answers questions easily, her dark eyes shining with the light of certainty, her hands moving expressively to emphasize each point. She's wearing a simple sari and her hair is tied back in a bun.

Someone else asks a question. Meanwhile, a young European woman on my left is doing simultaneous translation into French, speaking rapidly and softly into a microphone.

Is it a recording, or is Paris listening? Either way, it looks like hard work.

The sun is beginning to set and a mosquito bites my right foot. I remove a large tube of Odomos from of my bag and cover my feet with cream. Atmananda, I notice, is also being bitten because he is fidgeting with his feet – as meditatively as possible, of course.

I try to flash the Odomos tube at him, but he doesn't seem to notice. Instead, he tucks one foot up inside his orange robe and leaves the other as mosquito dessert.

Devaki is straightforward and traditional. Her basic message is the *bhakti* manifesto: Surrender at the feet of your guru. This is what she did with Yogi Ramsuratkumar and he, in turn, gave all credit for his teachings to "the Father," which was his name for God or the Self.

Since Devaki is doing all the talking, I slowly begin to understand the situation. Atmananda likes to introduce his followers to as wide a range of spiritual views as possible. He's not here to talk. He's here to support Devaki while she shares her vision.

He did a similar thing with Nochur, the Brahmin scholar, going every morning to Nochur's discourses on Ramana Maharshi and studiously taking notes, so he could pass on any spiritual gems to his followers.

I'm beginning to warm to Atmananda. He may be a

scholar, he may be an intellectual, he may like to toss around spiritual concepts like other people swap Instagram photos, but he's sincere, humble and willing to learn from anyone.

He's also quietly determined. Two days ago, he gave Satsang on a rooftop while, down below, a local funeral was in progress, which included some of the loudest drumming I have ever heard in my life plus sustained bursts of firecrackers. The noise was deafening, but all Atmananda did was ask his sound engineer to turn up the volume of his microphone and carried on. He did pause for the firecrackers, though. They were ear-splitting.

Rumour has it that Atmananda has a guru, deep in the Himalayas, who runs a super-strict ashram, with no tourists allowed. Just to get in, you need to commit to four hours of silent meditation every day and to help with washing the dishes. Fortunately, I don't know the address.

Meanwhile, Devaki is talking about the consciousness of the holy mountain, Arunachala, as the manifestation of Shiva. Another question occurs to me and I raise my hand. Atmananda looks at me curiously, but says nothing.

"Do you think the mountain itself has consciousness or is it simply a reservoir for the combined consciousness of the hundreds of yogis and siddhas who have meditated there?" I ask.

"It is both," replies Devaki. She also talks about a fable in which Ramana, wandering on the mountain, one day finds a cave leading into a golden world inside which is so powerful and dazzling that, after exiting, he rolls a boulder across to conceal the entrance.

Why? To stop anyone else from entering, knowing that if they did, the power of the golden energy will completely destroy them. Wouldn't you know? We ordinary mortals miss out on all the fun.

It occurs to me that I might need a photo of Atmananda and Devaki, so I cautiously slide my mobile phone out of

Subhuti Anand Waight

my pocket, switch on the camera and take a couple of shots. The guy next to me sees everything, but says nothing. Very tolerant, these people.

Question time winds to an end. Atmananda thanks Devaki, gives a her a gift and a donation, and the meeting breaks up.

"Hello, how did you get in?" asks a white clad American woman, whom I know works closely with Atmananda. She'd been sitting behind me the whole time.

Ooops! I give her a weak smile. "I thought it was a public meeting," I reply, sheepishly.

She smiles and says nothing.

I stroll over to Gayatri.

"I need food," she says.

"Me too," I say and off we go on her ancient scooter to a nearby restaurant: a tasty palak paneer for me and masala uttapam for her.

Alas, Gayatri will soon be leaving for Amma's ashram in Kerala and my best Tiru guide will be gone.

IN A FIELD OF ITS OWN

It's after sunset and I'm enjoying a delicious apple crumble with mango ice cream. At the same time, I need to keep an eye on the time because at seven o'clock I will need to be upstairs, ready for the movie.

When I do ascend to the open roof, I see a gorgeous sight: a big orange-coloured full moon, rising in the east, with Mount Arunachala looming as a dark, massive shadow to the north. It's a fabulous picture and I do my best to capture the moment with my mobile.

At seven, Matt, one of the cooks from the vegan restaurant downstairs, introduces us to the movie he helped to make. It's about a spiritual teacher called Adi Da Samraj, also known by many other names, including Baba Free John.

I knew about Da Free John – another name he adopted –

                    Subhuti Anand Waight

long ago, in the Seventies and Eighties, and probably would have checked him out, but we were usually never on the same continent at the same time. And besides, after I met Osho in 1976, I pretty much lost interest in everybody else on the spiritual circuit.

It has been through the inspiration of Adi Da that Matt, his companion Deb, and another couple, Donald and Roos, have created 'Da Mantra,' an all-vegan restaurant that looks beautiful, feels beautiful and for sure tastes beautiful.

'Da Mantra' stands alone in a field. Maybe that's a suitable metaphor because there's nothing else like it in Tiru. The food is fantastic and although I can't afford to eat here that often – the prices are a little high for my modest budget – I do so whenever I can.

Whether it's the spaghetti, the falafel, or the home style curry, the portions are huge. In fact, on a couple of occasions I've shared a single meal with a friend and it's been more than enough for both of us. But I can't share the apple crumble. Oh no, that needs to be all mine.

Frequently, there is evening entertainment. Last Sunday night, for example, a *bhajan* singer called Ganga Ma, a follower of Atmananda, gave a wonderful concert, bringing together about 50 people in graceful, harmonious chanting.

As yet, I don't know whether the aim of 'Da Mantra' is to share the vision of Adi Da or to promote veganism as a way of life – maybe both. But both are done in a low-key way, without any kind of fanaticism. The vegan food speaks for itself and the movie is only for those who are interested.

As I watch the movie, I see that Adi Da conveys the same message as Osho, Ramana and all mystics: we are living a dream existence under the illusion that we are separate. When we awaken to what Adi Da calls 'The Bright,' we realize that we are, and have always been, pure consciousness. The movie ends with Adi Da's departure from the body in 2008, at his retreat centre on an island in Fiji.

Afterwards, when I ask about the link between Adi Da and veganism, Matt tells me the mystic was keen on discovering the healthiest diet for his disciples and, by extension, for the public in general. So, the restaurant is a way of sharing Adi Da's understanding that humans do better -- and are likely to be more aware and conscious – when they don't eat animal products.

Just as an aside, I was on the Oregon Ranch with Osho, in the early Eighties, at a time when media-driven allegations accused Adi Da of practicing mind control and sexually abusing some of his followers. A friend of mine working in our PR department told me she got a call from one of the mystic's close associates seeking advice on how to deal with it.

Being with Osho, we, of course, were the experts in the controversy field. As I recall, my PR friend advised them to use this opportunity, presented by so much publicity, to get their own message across, and wished them good luck.

'Da Mantra' is coming to the end of its first full season. It will shut down at the end of March and reopen in November.

"It's only when we go through our books in April that we'll see how we've been doing financially," says Debbie. Hopefully, they'll have managed sufficiently well to be opening again next season. They certainly seem to have an enthusiastic clientele.

Meanwhile, I'll enjoy the lingering taste of the apple crumble and wash it down with a few sips of a delightful ginger kambucha tea. Bon appetit!

Subhuti Anand Waight

GURUS AND GIRLFRIENDS

Melanie has been to bed with her guru. Even before it happened, she was referring to him, laughingly, as "my husband." At forty years old, with a good deal of life experience in her backpack, Melanie can hardly be said to be a classic #MeToo victim, although, to a degree, she does fit the category.

"From the moment I saw his photo, I felt pulled to him," she recalls, describing her affair with a man about ten years older than herself. "I wanted to meet him and I wanted to talk with him. It must have been obvious at that first Satsang because he told me he also wanted to talk with me. He invited me to dinner, and the following night we ended up in bed."

Melanie, who comes from London, explained that, at first it seemed like they were meeting as two mature adults, but soon she felt herself slipping into what she called "a victim space."

"I became the lost little girl and he was going to be my saviour, my spiritual daddy," she recalls. "But he wouldn't allow me to stay in that space. He kept pointing it out and that was how I managed to work through it."

Melanie is passionate about learning through life experience. Intensity shines in her eyes, as she sips her coffee and reviews her love affair.

"You can say he should not have allowed it, but I can't blame him," she says. "Because if things hadn't gone the way they did, I would never have had such an important learning experience."

Her guru has now shifted to Rishikesh and she's wondering whether to join him. She's hesitating. She doesn't feel it's the right time and anyway, she confides with a giggle, she's already met someone else – not a Satsang-giver but an Indian man who has the same kind of spiritual intensity.

"This time it's the heart. There's no sex involved. But you never know," she muses, "sex can always come into the picture. Then I'll have to decide if it's what I want."

These days, it seems everybody is on their way to Rishikesh. Another friend of mine, a few years older than Melanie, is going to participate in a retreat there with a Canadian mystic called John de Ruiter. In the past, he's often given Satsangs and led retreats in Tiru, but this year he's available only in Rishikesh.

I met John a long time ago, in the late Nineties when he was visiting the Osho Resort in Pune. We were starting to have a conversation, near the main gate, when an attractive young German woman interrupted us, looked John straight in the eyes and said, "I want to make love with you."

John seemed taken aback. "Oh," was all he managed to say. I was also taken aback. I'd been attracted to this woman

     Subhuti Anand Waight

and felt that a slow, gradual approach was needed. Yet, here she was, openly offering herself as a way to get close to a guru-like figure.

As far as I know, the connection wasn't pursued because John was called to the Reception Office and told he couldn't stay. Why not? Well, not because of any sexual impropriety. The Resort officials were concerned he'd use the place as a recruiting ground to get more followers and that was not permitted. This was a general policy towards gurus, not specific to de Ruiter.

About 15 years later, after John had gained an international following, he featured in a major scandal that attracted a great deal of media attention, especially in Edmonton, Canada, where his headquarters was located. Two beautiful sisters, whose father had financially supported John, brought a civil lawsuit against their guru, claiming he'd seduced them both into a secret triangular affair while he continued living with his wife.

According to a national newspaper report, one of the women also alleged that de Ruiter publicly preached a message of marital fidelity and honesty while at the same time privately telling her to submit to him because it was God's will. Additional revelations about affairs with other women in the community surfaced shortly afterwards.

It was a big, bad mess. But it seems that John has survived because he is still offering meditation retreats. That's where my friend is headed.

For me, there are a few issues here:

First, as we know, the rise of the #MeToo movement has spotlighted the temptation for men in positions of power to sexually exploit women who work for them as employees or who come to them seeking guidance or who devote themselves as followers.

This is a huge issue and has unearthed misconduct in the spiritual world as well as everywhere else. The more understood these tendencies are, the better prepared and protected women will be.

Second, there is a sub-category in which, rather like groupies chasing rock stars, some women are willing to use their sexuality to gain personal access to male spiritual teachers. This is a grey area because, while there is no coercion, no pressure, there is a still degree of exploitation – maybe on both sides.

Third, it seems to me that in these modern, liberated times there is no need for hypocrisy. To preach celibacy and marital fidelity to others, while secretly enjoying sexual freedom yourself, is just plain mean.

If you believe in sexual freedom, why not let everyone join the party? That's what happened back in the Seventies in Pune. We were known worldwide as "the free love ashram" where women and men were encouraged to explore their sexual energy, while at the same time being invited to dive deeply into meditation.

Osho's message to the world was: celibacy and fidelity have nothing to do with spirituality and meditation, sex should be a playful affair, and two people should stay together only as long as they are in love.

Therefore, all spiritual teachers kindly note my request: have the guts, like we did, to be real. Preach what you live, live what you preach. If you're not brahmacharya, or celibate, don't claim that you are. If you advocate honesty, start in your own backyard.

Now, having said this, I need to add another dimension that's going to sound weird, but which, in my personal observation, is true: You don't need to be a saint to help people. You can lie, steal, cheat, be a hypocrite, a male chauvinist pig, or, in the reverse case, a female pain in the ass.

I'm not saying you should be any of these things. I'm not saying these qualities are laudable or excusable. I'm simply saying that spirituality is a totally different ballgame to conventional moral behaviour. The two don't meet.

In her book, *Holy Hell: A Memoir of Faith, Devotion and Pure Madness,* author Gail Tredwell looked behind the motherly image of Amma, the hugging saint, and caused a major international scandal with her allegations of abusive behaviour.

Tredwell's reports may be accurate, but they don't alter the fact that Amma is a powerhouse of cosmic energy, who can hug the whole world and give thousands of people a taste of divine love.

You get my point? An attempt last year by an anti-cult crusader to discredit Mooji as a spiritual teacher may have been based partly on facts, but Mooji's Satsangs will still benefit the people who go to them. And that's why an intelligent woman, like my friend, who is fully aware of John de Ruiter's scandal story, still chooses to go to his retreat, to enjoy the states of universal consciousness he seems capable of sharing.

Let me repeat, with added emphasis, I'm not saying this to provide justification for abusive behaviour. Not at all. But reality is reality. The plain fact is: you can't use a moral code to measure a spiritual phenomenon.

Well-intentioned magazines who publish point-by-point advice to help you avoid falling prey to spiritual exploitation are wasting their time. Someone can tick all the boxes and turn out to be a complete dud, or, more likely, a skilful deceiver.

So, what's left? What it comes down to, in the end, is that like Melanie, you have to make your own decision. Based on what you are experiencing in somebody's presence, you need to decide whether it's okay to be with that person – and in what way.

Moral issues may play a role in your decision; your personal preferences may also be a factor, and, in addition, spiritual experiences will have their own, distinct and separate part to play. Don't expect it all to make sense.

If you start asking questions like, "This guy seems like such an asshole, so how can he open my third eye?" you may wind up with a headache because the answer may not fit with your ideas.

It's you who has to decide. Other people may agree or disagree with you. Society may think you're nuts. That's not the point. In the end, it's down to you, and you alone.

The responsibility, my friend, is all yours. That's the risk, and that's your freedom.

                    Subhuti Anand Waight

NEARLY MEETING DEATH

body dies.' And I, at once dramatized the occurrence of death. I lay with my limbs stretched out stiff as though *rigor mortis* had set in and imitated a corpse so as to give greater reality to the enquiry. I held my breath and kept my lips tightly closed, so that no sound could escape, so that neither the word 'I' nor any other word could be uttered. 'Well then,' I said to myself, 'this body

He was doing his best to become enlightened but the cleaning lady stopped him. When I saw the whole thing happen, it made me smile: a neat illustration of how the mundane world can create problems for a seeker of truth.

It was mid-morning in the Ramana Ashram. I had entered with no particular purpose in mind, just a desire to be here and enjoy the quiet atmosphere.

Going up the steps by the office, on the ashram's main walkway, I turned left into the first meditation hall, where Ramana would sometimes sit with his disciples and which now acts as a kind of ante room to his mother's samadhi.

On one wall, there is a large inscription, describing one of the critical stages in Ramana's spiritual development: his near-death experience at the age of sixteen:

"The shock of the fear of death drove my mind inwards and I said to myself, mentally, without actually feeling the words: 'Now death has come, what does it mean? What is it that is dying? This body dies.' And I at once dramatized the occurrence of death. I law with my limbs stretched out stiff as though rigor mortis had set in and imitated a corpse so as to give greater reality to the inquiry...."

To give such prominence to this narrative clearly underlined the importance Ramana's experience had been given by the ashram authorities, perhaps by Ramana himself.

It was at this point I noticed a young Western man lying on his back, close to the wall on the other side of the hall. He was not sleeping, nor relaxing, but lying quite stiffly and it was obvious to me that he was exploring the same experiment: he wanted to use Ramana's words to see if he could at least capture the flavour of Ramana's inquiry into death.

But, alas, it was not to be. A middle-aged Indian woman, who'd been tidying up some flowers that had been laid as offerings in another part of the hall, also noticed him. She was clearly part of the staff and was not about to let anyone lie down in here which, in her eyes, was seen as a mark of disrespect.

She walked across the hall, stood over the young man and said, "Please sit up!"

He must have known she was talking to him, but, in a vain effort to maintain his inquiry, he continued lying as he was, with his eyes tightly closed. After all, in such a situation one might say to oneself: if the real challenge is death, what can a trivial encounter with a cleaning lady matter?

But she was not to be denied. "Sit up!" she exclaimed. "Lying down is not allowed in here!"

Reluctantly, the young man gave in. He sat up, shifted himself into a lotus position, stayed for a few more minutes, but then gave up his attempt at meditation and walked out. The moment had passed and his encounter with death had not been the intense experience for which he'd hoped.

This little incident makes me wonder: if someone today, walking on the mountain, comes across someone like Ramana,

    Subhuti Anand Waight

sitting alone, doing nothing, would he immediately pull out his mobile, call an ambulance, and say "Come soon! There's a guy here suffering from dehydration and disorientation – he doesn't seem to know who he is!"

THE LAST MOUNTAIN CLIMB

It's nearly time to go. I can feel it. I could stay on, but I know the heat will soon become intolerable without air conditioning and that, for me, is no pleasure. AC means spending more and more time indoors, trapped in an artificial pocket of coolness.

But Darshan hasn't climbed to the Arunachala caves yet, on this visit, and so, before she leaves, she invites me to accompany her. My cough is stubbornly persisting, but I feel strong enough to go with her.

When I suggest starting out at 7:00 am, she gives me a smile and an old-fashioned look.

"How about 8:30?" she replies. She doesn't want to miss the luxury breakfast at her hotel.

At 8:25 she's waiting for me just inside the gates of Ramana Ashram and together we walk through, using the side route so we don't have to take off our shoes.

As we approach the ashram's rear gate, I see several beggars waiting to greet us, to whom I offer a friendly namasté, while leaving their hands empty. After 44 years in India, I am immune to their entreaties.

Soon we pass the painting of Ramana sitting in meditation, surrounded by nature – the reforestation appeal for funding.

"We can rest whenever you like," says Darshan and this we do often. It's nice, actually, to climb this way, slowly, relaxed, without being focused on getting to our destination.

But it's also true that I am noticeably weaker than when I climbed at the beginning of my visit. Being sick has taken its toll. I joke that I should have borrowed a stethoscope from some local medical centre, so she can listen to my chest.

"Well, you're not wheezing with your breathing," says my doctor friend, professionally, "And if you had pneumonia, you wouldn't have got this far up the hill. So, I'd say you're doing okay."

We continue to make steady progress, navigate our way through a small band of monkeys, then find ourselves at the rocky outcrop which offers the best lookout point. From here, we see Tiruvannamalai spread out below and hear the noise of car horns and throbbing motorbike engines drifting up towards to us.

Then it's a gentle downhill slope to the Skandasram cave which already has a fair number of visitors. Softly spoken greetings come our way from the custodians at the gate, who, I am sure, are hoping for a tip on our way out.

For a while, I enjoy sitting under the trees, but then Darshan invites me to join her inside the first doorway, leading to the cave, where there is a kind of balcony area for about a dozen people to sit.

Neither of us feel like going into the inner sanctum, the actual cave itself, which may contain a stronger energy, but is smaller, darker, and more cramped.

I like to rest here and be quiet, feeling somehow that I

am sinking gently into the mountain's energy field. To tell the truth, though, I get almost the same feeling when sitting in my room. The field, as I've said before, is bigger than the mountain.

With so many Westerners feeling drawn to Tiru, it's obvious I'm not the only one who is sensitive to this field. Just the other evening, I was talking with a young mother, who regularly comes to the ashram to enjoy the evening singing.

"No matter where I travel in the world, I always feel drawn to come back here," she reflected. "After a while, other places just start to feel…empty."

For me, there are other meditative energy fields, in various countries, but they're not that common, and most of them don't have this extensive reach.

After about an hour, Darshan and I are both ready for the downward journey. As we start back along the track, I look up at the sky. It's cloudy and this is keeping the temperature down to a very pleasant level.

"You know, this would be an ideal day to hike to the top of the mountain," I tell Darshan.

She doesn't look at the sky. She looks at me with the mock sternness of a doctor monitoring a reluctant patient.

"You're right," she says, "But just forget it! This is your doctor speaking!"

Halfway down, we pass a Danish friend, standing off to one side, among the rocks, talking to her mobile which she holds out before her with a selfie stick. Back home, she's a spiritual teacher and here, in this auspicious location, she must be creating a new video clip for her students – direct from Arunachala.

This is not a time to wave or attract her attention. Next, we encounter a young Indian family – father, mother, and two children – resting on their way up. The father looks at me with a slightly desperate expression.

"How far is it to the caves?" he asks. I'm not sure if it's the kids who are tired, or him.

"About twenty minutes," I assure him. "Just take it slowly, step by step. You'll make it."

We arrive at the ashram's back gate once more, walk through to the main road and seek refuge in a local coffee shop, rewarding ourselves with a relaxing gossip after our walk.

"You know, I think Osho was also teaching advaita," reflects Darshan. "He insisted on using his own forms of expression, but it's the same message."

I could see her point. "Yes, it's true," I agree. "But he didn't like using positive concepts like 'the Self,' because he knew we'd cling to them as a way of helping the ego to survive. That's why his last discourse series was titled *The Zen Manifesto: Freedom From ...Oneself.*"

"It's still about merging the little self with the absolute Self," muses Darshan.

"It's not about merging," I insist. "It's about disappearing!"

We look at each other, bow to each other's wisdom, accept our different ways of looking at things and laugh. We raise our cups in a playful salute, in recognition:

Two selves on our way to disappearing.